<u>DEMoNOCRACY</u>

and 

<u>Other Fishy Matters</u>

The True Story of the
Queensland Commercial Fishing Industry

Geoffrey G. T. Harrison

with Eunice C. Harrison

Published by Geoffrey G. T. Harrison and InHouse Publishing

Triton devours Crown of Thorns Starfish.

DEDICATION

I was born in York, England, and this book is a brief account of my work in the Queensland Public Service for almost 20 years. It also records some of my efforts to assist in the development of the Queensland Fishing Industry. It could not have been written without the devoted help of Eunice Cecelia, my wonderful wife, for her strength in supporting me through many difficult and stressful times, and her success in keeping all the important records of the period. Eunice also took on the huge task of editing my efforts in the unfamiliar task of authorship and correcting my numerous errors and omissions. If not for Eunice by my side for the last 56+ years, the fine detail and references recorded in these pages would not have been possible to achieve.

Our four children, Marissa Jean, Celia Mary, Adam Enright and Geoffrey Thomas Gerard shared our burden during their growing up years. They are now responsible adults of whom we are very proud. All of our family have excelled in their chosen careers – Geoffrey Jnr. (Radio), Adam (Computer Science), Celia Mary (Aged Care) and Marissa (Paediatric Nursing). I dedicate this book to Eunice and our family. Eunice was born in the Lady Bowen Hospital, Wickham Terrace, Brisbane, and we met in Ghana where Eunice was working in the Australian High Commission. I love them dearly and am very proud of them.

Geoffrey and Eunice at the Manly Boat Harbour in 2017.

*Geoffrey Thomas Gerard, Adam Enright, Celia Mary and
Marissa Jean in 1974.*

FOREWORD

Geoff Harrison Director of Fisheries for Queensland is a good guy. He is educated, honest, experienced, always professional and a good family man. His life in Australia was always devoted to the good of the fisheries, their long term management and sustainability – a long time before that became a glib term. I am grateful that he has written this small book to set the record straight in relation to some of the 'happenings' during his tour of duty in Queensland.

He came to Queensland via Ghana from the UK where he gained his qualifications. He had done a good job in Ghana and was invited to come to Queensland to head up the Queensland Fisheries Service, a role he was well qualified to carry out. When he arrived, things were not as they were portrayed to him – not the first time that had happened to someone of course.

USA one line specialist Yogi Berra once said 'When you meet a fork in the road, take it'. That is exactly what Geoff had to do. He was out in the colony and had a young family growing every day. He had to give it his best shot. It was never going to be easy and it wasn't. His is an interesting story, not atypical of happenings around that time.

His problems were two fold.

Firstly, he found himself in a situation in the Public Service where outsiders were despised, especially from the UK. (Poms) They surrounded him with persons less qualified and inexperienced. He had to fight for everything including a phone, office and legislation. 'Life was not meant to be easy'.

Secondly, the political context was erratic, confusing, often contradictory and difficult to understand. I myself was impacted by this more than once. As a member of the Ministerial Council on the Barrier Reef, Premier Bjelke-Petersen sacked me for supporting the declaration of stage two of the Great Barrier Reef Management plan which I did on the advice of the Director General of the Premiers Department who was sitting beside me at the meeting. In six months time they did it anyway.

The politics surrounded the Drilling of the Great Barrier Reef, the impacts of farming on runoff, clearing of marine habitats, Crown of Thorns starfish etc. Bjelke-Petersen was very strident on these issues and Geoff said his piece on behalf of Fisheries conservation as he should and was isolated as a result.

Queensland Fisheries would have been better off today if the Government had acted on his professional advice.

Australians think there is a plentiful fishery resource here but plentiful it is not, which is due to the ocean current patterns. So they needed and still need careful management if they are to survive.

Geoff Harrison did his bit for the Fisheries and did it well. This is his story.

Novelist Leo Tolstoy in his novel 'The Death of Ivan Ilyich' describes his character asking the question at the end of his life 'I wonder if my life has been wrong?' This is a good question for all of us.

Geoff Harrison's life was for the Fisheries. His life has been right.

To those who have an interest in Fishery Management, it is a worthwhile read.

The Honourable Michael J. Ahern AO

Queensland Premier and
Treasurer and Minister for
State Development and
the Arts 1987-89

Mr Ahern served in the Queensland Parliament for 22 years as the Member for Landsborough. He was highly regarded as a Minister from his first Ministerial appointment as Minister for Primary Industries and later other portfolios including Industry, Small Business and Technology; Health and Environment; and State Development.

PREFACE

Writing a book, however short it may be, is not an easy task unless the motivation exists.

In my case, I had a triad of causes to air and felt that there was a public need to air them.

In February 1963, I was recruited from overseas following National advertising. There was no suitably trained applicant with experience in commercial fisheries within the State Public Service.

After my appointment, I discovered that I was being blocked by senior Public Servants in many things I attempted to do. Lacking up to date legislation, staff and facilities I could achieve little; but I could cop the blame.

I was given inadequate staff to share my load. It was only in special circumstances that I was able to recruit new staff, until Fisheries was transferred to the Department of Primary Industries. The position eased somewhat in DPI.

Eventually, I was removed from my position as the Officer-in-Charge of Queensland Fisheries, without any reason being given.

Cronyism was at the root of my problems – I was not "ONE OF US".

Democracy in Queensland is not working. A politicised bureaucracy, combined with a tightly controlled party-political system, helped along by cronyism, has ensured the perpetuation of DEMonOCRACY instead of DEMOCRACY.

Geoffrey Harrison arrived in Queensland in 1963.

Contents

CHAPTER 1

HM COLONIAL SERVICE (Ghana)

We all have to make choices in life and in 1962 I was faced with what was probably the most momentous decision of my life. After 13 years' service in Fisheries in Ghana (formerly the Gold Coast), a country in West Africa, where I became the Head of Fisheries, I had to decide whether to work in Peru, South America (which job I had accepted); Victoria in Australia; or in Queensland. Fortunately, I changed my mind about working in South America, because the Fisheries project there and most of the town were wiped out by an earthquake soon afterwards.

The reason for my departure from Ghana, after 13 years in HM Colonial Service, was that the country had become independent, and I was required to train a Ghanaian to take charge of the Fisheries Department. Furthermore, the retiring age from Ghana was 45 years for health reasons. Yellow fever and malaria were killers. White people who continued to serve for long after reaching the age of 45 rarely survived to enjoy more than three years of retirement.

I enjoyed my work in Ghana and the Ghanaians looked after me very well. I was adequately compensated for loss of career, and I selected Queensland for my next career opportunity.

I met the President of Ghana, Dr. Kwame Nkrumah, on many occasions, who was interested in my work. Fish was a major source of protein food for the people. The rearing of cattle was restricted due to the prevalence of the Tsetse fly in the forest areas.

His Excellency President Kwame Nkrumah talking with Geoffrey on Christiansborg beach.

I was presented to His Royal Highness Prince Philip by His Excellency the President on the beach near Christiansborg Castle, where we demonstrated the pioneer use of outboard motors on fishing canoes.

His Royal Highness Prince Philip, Geoffrey Harrison and His Excellency President Kwame Nkrumah (1959).

My deputy, Gordon Rawson, succeeded in making a simple clamp to fix the outboard motor to a canoe, which could be made by the local blacksmith and was strong enough to withstand the violent surf. This was a very successful project that trebled the fishermen's incomes.

I came to Brisbane from Ghana for an interview, and then returned to Ghana, at no charge to the Queensland Government. I was told the job would be a challenge (how was I to know that the people would be the challenge, not the job)? I understood that as Chief Inspector of Fisheries and Senior Biologist, I was to be the most senior Fisheries Officer in Queensland, and that I was expected to put all Fisheries matters, except the Fish Board, under the one umbrella, for the first time. I was the umbrella. At the interview I understood my appointment was subject to three conditions:

(1) That I join a registered industrial Union,
(2) That I pass a medical examination, and
(3) That I agree to stay five years.

I guaranteed to fulfil these requirements.

My degree is in chemistry. I served in the Royal Air Force from 14thOctober 1941 to 5th July 1946, following a year spent in the Home Guard. My service record said:

"An outstanding N.C.O. with a sound record. His technical ability is above average and during the last few months while he has been in charge of a section, he has displayed great ability as an organiser."

I completed a training course in Fisheries Management that was organised in Denmark by the Food and Agriculture Organisation of the United Nations, and the Danish Government, followed by courses in food canning, echo sounders and marine engines in the United Kingdom.

Fisheries Management Course in Denmark.

Some of my Fisheries staff in Ghana-Farewell to Geoffrey, Gordon Rawson, and to Eunice.

Fisheries officers and local officials in Accra.

When I retired in August 1962, as Head of the Department of Fisheries in Ghana, I had a staff of about 300 including nine graduate scientists, mainly Biologists. I administered an industry landing approximately as much fish each year as the total catch of Australia at the time I was appointed here.

During my thirteen years' service in Fisheries in Ghana I gained valuable managerial and technical experience. I was also involved in the design of the fishing harbours at Tema and Elmina, and I had the honour to talk about Tema to Her Majesty Queen Elizabeth II and Prince Philip.

CHAPTER 2

THE PIONEER

I claim to be the Pioneer of the Queensland Commercial Fishing Industry.

The Honourable Mike Ahern, when Queensland Minister responsible for Fisheries, said, inter alia, in relation to "Marine Science Policy in Queensland":

> "Despite the fact that fisheries departments as a group are one of the largest employers of graduate Biologists in the country, it is a pity that marine biological courses in the various universities in Australia have not been more strongly oriented towards Fisheries.

> To many people, the term Fisheries Scientist is synonymous with Marine Biologist. Such an attitude is understandable in view of the past history of Fisheries in this country.

> Fisheries Science deals with Fisheries, not just the animals which are the target of those Fisheries. The most vital parameter of a Fisheries Scientist's calculations is not some biological property of a fish but a variable called fishing effort, a curious combination

of boat and gear characteristics and use, fish behaviour and fishermen's know-how.

As a result, the ideal Fisheries Scientist needs to be part-biologist, part-economist, part-gear technologist and part-sociologist. Some people say he needs to be part-lawyer as well, as the end product of his labours is frequently some form of restrictive legislation."

I would add that Fisheries Management involves the exercise of Statutory Legal Powers so as to conserve a public resource and to share it equitably and fairly between the community groups involved.

The ideal Fisheries Manager also needs to be experienced in other fields such as fishing vessel design, fish processing, marketing, and the needs of anglers as well as the general community. These fields of knowledge are just as important as biological and statistical studies of the actual fish resources for which he holds responsibility.

Decisions must often be made which are based on inadequate data because catch and effort statistics take years to collect and assessment of the fish stock is also a long-term project. A Fisheries Manager's decisions are often based on his wide experience in this work and subject to revision as data accumulates. It is only by these "educated guesses" that the Fisheries resources can be preserved, and over-investment, subsequent expensive buy-back of excess licences, and hardship among the fishermen can be minimised.

A Fisheries Manager acquires these skills, partly through formal training, mainly through long experience. His knowledge of the community and the actual fishermen, amateur and professional, can only be gleaned from personal contacts and from a well trained cadre of field officers or inspectors at work in each area. These are not primarily enforcement officers but public relations experts. I was well equipped in experience, but mostly I was deprived of such trained field staff in Queensland.

My only source of community information was my own personal contacts in Queensland and my Senior Inspector, Arthur Rowell, whose knowledge of the old net fishing methods was comprehensive, but lacked experience in modern fishing.

The Fishing Industry was just developing from the artisanal to the industrial stage in Queensland when I arrived. The Moreton Bay and East Coast prawn fisheries were growing fast and uncontrolled. Offshore the mackerel fishery had been expanded by a faulty marketing system, which filled the cold stores with poor quality fish. There were no research or survey facilities and the fishermen had no effective representation. Fisheries legislation was obsolescent.

A very good but dated report on Queensland Fisheries by Saville-Kent, and reports on pearling, oyster culture, and whaling (which had just ceased at Tangalooma) were available in the Fisheries Library. This Library was the best resource available to me at the time. The Commonwealth Government had conducted a trawl survey on the East Coast during the career of my predecessor the Government Ichthyologist, Tom Marshall, which led fishermen into the ocean prawn fishery. I had a long hard road to travel.

How could I possibly have known then that I would spend approximately the last seven years of my service in Queensland in a general office, in a corner behind a screen, in the Department of

Aboriginal and Islanders Advancement with no staff, no budget, no explanation, and, for a long time, no telephone?

This is my story. I am writing it because I believe it is my duty to write it, in the public interest, setting out what happened to me, the huge cost to the State of Queensland and to the Fishing Industry.

Many of my proposals to develop Queensland Fisheries were blocked over several years, at a great cost to taxpayers. I am of the opinion that this was done in order to force my resignation, and that one of the reasons for this was because I was appointed from "Outside" to a senior position in Queensland.

I believe I am the Longest Survivor of the System - almost 20 years. After all, Honest Cop, Ray Whitrod, survived only approximately 7 years.

In spite of this blocking, I claim to be the Pioneer of the Queensland Commercial Fishing Industry. On 21st March 2005, my wife and I had a lengthy interview with the Principal Legal Officer, Department of Primary Industries and Fisheries, Kristian Holz, who examined a complete record of my service in Queensland Fisheries.

Mr. Holz turned to me and said, "You are the Pioneer of the Queensland Commercial Fishing Industry." I replied "Yes", and added that the East Coast prawn fishery was just starting, but there was no semblance of any Government organisation to oversee the fishery.

We told Mr. Holz that in 1961 we visited Queensland House in London and enquired about Fisheries Development in Queensland. The only Fisheries material they were able to produce were old annual reports from the Queensland Fish Board listing the quantities of fish sold at auction.

I retired from the Queensland Public Service on the 6th August 1982, with a clean record and without any disciplinary action. Up till that time my attitude was "I was brought here to do a job and I will do it in spite of THEM." In the end the disease of CRONYISM defeated me. I said at the time of leaving on 27th May 1975, "I am at the end of the road after almost 13 years of trying."

My first office in the Department of Harbours & Marine.

CHAPTER 3

HARBOURS & MARINE

I commenced duty as The Chief Inspector of Fisheries and Senior Biologist in the Department of Harbours and Marine on 28th February 1963, and I discovered that there was no effective fisheries organisation at all. Previously, fisheries administration, enforcement and marketing had been separated and handled by different people. There was no sign of Fisheries Management.

The Department Head, Arthur James Peel, had told me at my interview that I faced a challenge, and I thought that I would receive some support. I was wrong. My staff comprised two Marine Biologists Ernest Morgan Grant and Noel Melville Haysom, who had worked in the Department approximately 13 and 12 years respectively. They had no defined duties. One was in an unclassified position in the Public Service and the other was on a temporary appointment. I took action to have them appointed to a scientific grade in the Public Service in which they would have promotion prospects.

My other staff consisted of a Senior Inspector of Fisheries, Arthur Rowell, and ten Inspectors to cover thousands of miles of coastline, the Great Barrier Reef, and all the rivers of Queensland. The Inspectors of Fisheries were not trained in Fisheries matters, but were boatmen employed by the Harbour Masters at the various ports and self-trained by working in their districts.

Previously, the Portmaster, Captain Masterman, had been in charge of the Department; the Secretary, Eric Coulter, handled the administration; the Senior Inspector of Fisheries, Arthur Rowell, did the field work; and the Government Ichthyologist, Tom Marshall, assisted by two Marine Biologists were advisers with no statutory duties, who busied themselves with taxonomy and general correspondence. No thought was given to the need for scientific work, or any other matters pertaining to commercial fishing such as resource management.

The Fisheries office consisted of an annexe at the back of the building which housed the Department of Harbours and Marine. My first office was situated adjacent to a stairwell, and also housed a large taxonomic collection and a desk used by a clerical assistant, who volunteered to do my typing when I was unable to access the typing pool. The two Marine Biologists occupied a glass conservatory, which also served as a taxonomic laboratory. Outside was a wharf used by two steam tugs and sundry boats. It was also used as storage for numerous steel buoys. It was dusty and noisy.

Noel Haysom said in "Trawlers, Trollers and Trepangers," which he authored and which was published in 2001 by the Department of Primary Industries, as follows –

"We were both graduates of the University of Queensland. Neither of us, in the early days of our employment, did very much of what might be regarded as serious research, apart from a few taxonomic problems. We were expected to be jacks-of-all-trades, and our roles were very akin to that of general practitioners in the medical world. A problem would arise, one or both of us would be sent off to do a quick investigation and diagnosis, to be followed by an internal report and recommendation. We would then, usually, be thanked and set off to investigate the next urgent problem, with little opportunity to write up or publish results in a scientific journal."

To make matters worse, amongst the files piled up on my desk awaiting my arrival were three which demanded urgent and major attention. These files, which had been ignored, or set aside to await my arrival in Queensland, were as follows:

Firstly, there were several reports concerning an abundance of prawns in the Gulf of Carpentaria which demanded urgent attention over the next four years, and which also led to great legal and political turmoil later;

Secondly, reports that the coral was being destroyed on the Green Island Reef by a giant starfish, causing panic in the tourist trade, which is so important to Queensland;

Thirdly, I discovered to my horror that I was required to attend a conference of Australian Fisheries Officers in the near future, and to represent Queensland. I would then be required to give advice to my Minister, who would attend the Fisheries Council meeting," which followed the officers' conference.

These files were obviously neglected for a long time and in some cases for several months. I wondered what the Fisheries staff had been doing prior to my arrival. I discovered that it was not just an uphill battle so much as a solo expedition up Everest. I had no effective support from my senior staff who resented my appointment from "Outside" Queensland. I was brought here, from "Outside", because there was no person available in the Public Service to take charge of Fisheries in Queensland, who was trained and experienced as a Fisheries Manager – and there were other reasons. I was selected from eight applicants.

The position which I had accepted had been represented to me as a consolidation of all responsibility for Fisheries matters into one person, except the Fish Board. (I was later told to keep my nose out of the Fish Board).

I had assumed, quite wrongly as it turned out, that being the first officer appointed to a new position, I would be given the necessary support in staff and facilities. I soon discovered that this was not the case.

To make matters worse I had agreed, trustingly, to pay the air fares to Brisbane for me and my wife which I understood would be refunded on arrival. When I took up duty, my Department Head refused to pay up until I signed a four and a half foolscap page contract, none of which had been explained to me when I visited Queensland from Ghana for an interview at my own expense.

Also, I made no claims for conveyance and other expenses, except for two air fares, when I travelled from Ghana to Brisbane to take up duty in 1963 in the Department of Harbours and Marine.

Although I objected to signing this Deed after I took up duty, I was forced to sign it or lose all my money. It took me more than five months to have my fares refunded. When I asked for interest I was told that I shouldn't have taken so long to sign the Deed. (I particularly objected to Clause 7 whereby if I failed for **any** reason to complete the **whole** of my probationary period and the confirmed appointment period then I, and presumably my estate, would be required to refund the **full amount** to Government).

Section 81 (11) of the Public Service Regulations of 1958 - "The Public Service Acts, 1922 to 1965", New Appointees, states that in regard to the cost of conveyance and other expenses a person, upon appointment to the Public Service shall be paid such amount………….."

"Public Service Acts 1922-1978", Section 18 (3) (IV) Special Cases states – "If in a special case it appears expedient in the interests of the Public Service to appoint to the Public Service a person who is not in the Service, the Governor in Council may, on the recommendation of the Board, appoint such person without examination, and also, if so recommended, without probation.

No such appointment shall, however, be made until the Board has certified that in its opinion there is no person available in the Service for such appointment who is capable of filling the office to which it is proposed that the appointment shall be made."

Later I took leave to visit my family in England in 1967. I became ill on the trip, supplied three medical certificates and applied for some of my accrued sick leave. I was given three weeks' leave without pay. This was the last occasion on which I saw my Mother.

This was my introduction to sunny Queensland. My wife and I were locked in as we had committed our assets to building our home, and we had a young family. I had to make it work.

My Head of Department had no knowledge of the Fishing Industry. During my first week I quickly skimmed through all the files, picking out those which could not wait, including the three I have already spoken about. I requested my two Biologists to start dealing with the remaining files. They protested, saying this was not scientific work.

Eventually when I complained to my Head of Department, I was told "This is your problem". It should be noted that my Head of Department exercised the disciplinary powers under the Public Service Act. I did not. I am not aware of any action he took to resolve the matter.

After a few months I was able to take over a temporary wing of the Harbours and Marine building which had become vacant. This gave us adequate accommodation, but I suffered from the noise of barnacles being chipped from steel buoys with hammers on the wharf outside my window for long periods, and often it was difficult to speak on the telephone.

I set out with my Senior Inspector, Arthur Rowell, on a series of hurried tours around Queensland meeting with fishermen in all the ports. I also visited Green Island on the Great Barrier Reef and Karumba in the Gulf of Carpentaria.

On my return from these trips I arranged that my Assistant Biologist, Noel Haysom, should visit Green Island regarding the Crown of Thorns Starfish problem and give me a brief report.

Meanwhile, I made contact with the Head of the Commonwealth Fisheries Department, Cedric Setter, and the Director of the Fisheries Division of the Commonwealth Scientific and Industrial Research Organisation (CSIRO), Dr. Geoffrey Kesteven. Cedric Setter and Geoff Kesteven soon became friends, the only friends on whom I could rely, apart from my wife and family. I arranged meetings with these men in Sydney and Canberra to discuss the possibility of a joint survey of the prawn resources of the Gulf of Carpentaria.

Cedric Setter and Geoffrey Harrison.

The attitude of the Director of the Department of Harbours and Marine to research was that it should be carried out by the CSIRO, and financed jointly and equally by the Commonwealth and the State Government. It was my responsibility to persuade the Commonwealth officer to agree to fund any project that I wanted to implement. This policy prevented me from employing research staff or conducting independent scientific research in Queensland. There was to be no permanent fisheries research effort in Queensland at that time. This unwieldy process was the best that I could achieve after much discussion.

Arthur James Peel was an excellent Auditor and Accountant, with no knowledge in the Fisheries field. The Department of Harbours and Marine was a revenue collecting Department involved in Ports, Shipping and Navigation. Fisheries, which should have been in a scientific environment, did not belong in this Department. It should have been an independent Department or a part of a Department with a strong scientific structure.

CHAPTER 4

GULF of CARPENTARIA

PRAWN SURVEY.

After I had completed these preliminary tasks, I concentrated my efforts on organising a survey of the prawn resources of the Gulf of Carpentaria. I chartered a fishing vessel, reached agreement with a private company to co-operate in the survey and arranged with the CSIRO and the Commonwealth Government Fisheries Officers to do the survey. I set up a committee, which I chaired, to supervise the work. Dr. Ian Munro, the project leader, was a senior research officer with CSIRO. He did a mighty job under difficult conditions. I recruited a technical assistant to work on the survey with Noel Haysom as the State contribution to the staff for a few months. George Bee, a young man, fresh from England, found the conditions in the north of Queensland difficult, but working under Ian Munro gave him valuable experience.

The survey lasted two years and two months. It located a very large resource of banana prawns, as well as a similar resource of tiger and endeavour prawns. It was obvious that these prawn resources, particularly the banana prawns, **demanded** action to manage and control the development of the fishery. Most of these prawns were found as adults in waters outside the control of the State in Commonwealth or International waters, which made management difficult. The banana prawns occurred, in a short season, following the rains, in very concentrated shoals called "boils". Most of the time spent at sea by the boats was used in searching, and very little in catching the prawns.

When a "boil" was found the daylight fishing operation was soon over and the first boats on the scene were quickly loaded. The boats needed a very large chilling or freezing capacity so as to accommodate the large catch rate. Banana prawns were highly vulnerable to economic overfishing, since the stock appeared to be controlled mainly by the rains in the river catchments. In addition, there were indications that the stocks would be quickly and fully exploited due to their vulnerable exposure in concentrated shoals.

Catch per boat was likely to be determined by the number of boats sharing a shoal, or first boat on the scene.

The overall value of the banana prawn catch depends upon the quantity of prawns available and their size at capture. The quantity of prawns is largely a function of the capacity of the rivers to hold and support juveniles, and the strength of the annual rains to wash them out. The size at capture depends upon the time the prawns are captured after entering the sea. The number of prawns is therefore relatively stable. The value of the catch is determined by the size of the prawns landed (the processors want prawns large enough to be easily processed and sold). Therefore the trawlers must not start fishing until the prawns have grown to market size, a time which varies from year to year. The solution is to ban fishing until samples indicate that the prawns have reached market size (a closed season with variable opening date is appropriate). The behaviour of the prawns makes their capture rapid and efficient and each "boil" is shared by the boats on the spot. The total catch, being relatively stable in size and controlled by the monsoonal rains, is sufficient to support the profitable operation of only a limited number of boats and processors; therefore, in a remote area such as the Gulf of Carpentaria, a limit should be set on the number of each in each area to ensure a profitable operation is possible.

Obsolete Queensland legislation did not allow either of these controls to be implemented on the fishing grounds. The only possible option available to me was to limit the number of prawn landing bases for which Crown land might be made available. Action on this proposal was not implemented by the Queensland Government in spite of my numerous requests.

The tiger and endeavour prawns were spread over large areas of sea bed and were a night time fishery. The catch was proportional to the area swept by the nets and catch rates were similar to those found in the East Coast King Prawn Fishery. This resource seemed to be capable of sustaining a profitable operation for much of the year.

The two prawn fisheries of the Gulf area were so different in nature that I raised the matter of designing a suitable vessel. None of the existing fleet was adequate to handle banana prawn catches. A sub-committee was set up which included a Naval Architect, Ronald Wright, and Craig Mostyn of the Craig Mostyn Fishing

Company, to design a suitable vessel. Mr. Mostyn later built this. It was 70ft. in length with powerful refrigeration capable of handling banana prawns in brine tanks or tiger prawns in cartons in a blast freezer.

The management of the Gulf Prawn Fisheries and other Northern Fisheries in State, Commonwealth and International waters was obviously beyond the powers of any single Government. This problem was solved later by the establishment of the Northern Fisheries Research Committee. This was based on my recommendation at the Fisheries Officers' Conference. This Committee then became a forum for the discussion and resolution of Fisheries Management problems in waters from Broome to Bowen (refer to Chapter 10 - Fisheries Officers' Conference regarding the setting up of this committee).

The immediate problem was that this banana prawn fishery demanded control by a limited licence system and a closed season, which was impossible under the obsolete Queensland Fisheries Acts, 1957-62. It was possible only through new legislation by Queensland supported by mirror legislation by the Commonwealth. I had already reached verbal agreement on this with Commonwealth Fisheries officers and drafted suitable legislation, following which no action had been taken by Queensland to approach the Commonwealth formally.

At the end of the survey the Director of Commonwealth Fisheries, Cedric Setter and I drafted a joint report recommending alternate management measures in the Gulf area consisting of the allocation of Crown Land to only one company in each of six areas. The leases were to be restricted to full prawn processing and freezing facilities and not used merely for landing prawns into road transport for processing elsewhere. The submission also included the need for matching legislation by the Commonwealth and State Governments, and asked that the Queensland Government should make a formal request to the Commonwealth Government for this to be drafted. The report pointed out the need for infrastructure such as roads, water supply and power, particularly at Karumba. This joint committee report was submitted to my Head of Department in August 1966, but did not reach State Cabinet until 22nd November 1967. Cabinet then decided that no shore sites would be granted to prawn fishing companies at Karumba pending a further submission. By that time there were six applicants for land and many boats already fishing the area outside my control.

In 1968 I flew in a spotter aircraft, with door removed and me hanging out with a camera, suspended by my seat belt, to assess waterfront land that could be used for prawning bases.

I prepared a fresh Cabinet submission, supported by the same joint report from Cedric Setter and me, recommending once again the allocation of land to prawn processing companies (one in each area) to the exclusion of prawn trans-shipment depot operators. Trans-shipment depots transfer prawns in ice by road to processing plants elsewhere, reducing local employment and development as well as the quality of the final product.

The report also recommended that legislation should be prepared to manage the fishery by controlling the processing and landing of prawns by the prawning companies, and by mother ships (which process prawns on board). This report was handed to my Head of Department who referred it to the officers of the Treasury Department. It was rejected and re-drafted, reversing the recommendations on Trans-shipment depots made by me and Cedric Setter (Commonwealth Fisheries).

The re-drafted Cabinet submission completely ignored the need for mirror legislation, and it also misrepresented the joint recommendations of the Commonwealth and State Fisheries Officers by claiming that Cedric Setter and I agreed with it, knowing that, in fact, we disagreed. This brought about an exchange of letters between the Prime Minister and the Premier and eventually sparked action on legislation by Queensland.

Craig Mostyn Fishing Company had provided most of the infrastructure at Karumba, at great expense to them, together with six prawn trawlers which helped in the survey. The Company built a water supply tank and dam, an electricity supply, a supermarket and accommodation units as well as their prawn processing plant, jetty and fuelling facility. In addition the Company bought and renovated the Hotel. The Queensland Government, over a number of years, built a new access road to Karumba and sunk a bore which provided water laden with fluorine, which could not be used for drinking or prawn processing. The more expensive option of a pipeline from a weir on the Normanton road was long delayed.

This re-drafted Cabinet submission also glossed over the matter of giving Craig Mostyn some short term monopoly in return for his investment at Karumba. Markwell Fisheries received its lease and thus competed on highly favourable terms as a Trans-shipment Depot. Craig Mostyn was running a full processing plant at Karumba, having accepted the early assurances of some protection, which was not honoured.

Another submission on Gulf prawn management was prepared jointly by the Commonwealth Director of Fisheries and me, repeating the need to limit processing plants to one in each area, and to rejecting all trans-shipment type operations. The Trans-shipment Depot operated by Markwells, having been committed, was to be converted to full processing at Karumba when potable water supplies became available.

Further submissions by Cedric Setter and myself were then circulated to Cabinet on these lines in April 1969. The Under-Treasurer drafted yet another paper for the Queensland Cabinet, pointing out that the previous decisions could not be implemented due to lack of legislative power, which I already knew only too well, and to the failure of the Commonwealth to take necessary action. In fact, the Commonwealth had not been formally asked.

Actually, it was the Queensland bureaucrats blocking tactics, and their failure to allow me to amend the Fisheries Acts, that caused the problem.

This sorry story of bureaucratic blocking and delays, which I now believe was aimed at me to force my resignation, had a devastating effect on the Gulf Prawn Fishery. Numerous fishermen who took their vessels to the Gulf in good faith were unable to cover expenses, because of the large number of vessels fishing and sharing the available catch. As the most senior Fisheries officer in Queensland, the complaints from the fishermen landed on my desk.

I had first recommended the need for legislation and secured Commonwealth Fisheries Officers' verbal approval to similar legislation in 1968. This, however, required a formal request from the Queensland Government to the Commonwealth Government, which the bureaucrats refused to implement. At least six years were wasted as the result of this bureaucratic blocking and delay. The economics of banana prawn fishing in the Gulf demand restrictive management either of landing bases or of boats. The former was preferred at the time because legislation to provide for a limited entry fishery did not exist. No action was taken to apply my advice and I was helpless.

Cabinet then decided to accept no further responsibility in this matter. These Cabinet decisions were sent to the Commonwealth. The Prime Minister sent a telegraphed reply to the Queensland Premier proposing a special officers' meeting on 12th May 1969. This was a meeting I had requested over two years earlier to sort out the interlocked jurisdiction problem. The meeting was held and it was agreed that the Commonwealth Fisheries Act would be amended to clear the way for State licensing of processing plants. Amending legislation was passed by Commonwealth in October 1970, one year five months later, and the State Act followed in November 1974, after a **further delay of four years.**

> "The Courier-Mail", much later, on September 26th 1984, reporting on the Gulf of Carpentaria Prawn Fishery quoted Dave Mitchell, the Head of the Queensland Fish Management Authority, as saying that about one third of the trawlers now operating in the Gulf (260) would have to be excluded next year to make the fishery into a profitable operation. There were too many vessels in the fishery. A $5,000,000 licence buy-back scheme had been approved."

It would have been much less costly and less painful to the industry if my new Fisheries Act had been accepted when I first proposed it in the late 1960s. The consistent blocking and distortion of my proposals cost the fishermen and the State millions of dollars and, as the officer-in-charge, the buck stopped with me.

CHAPTER 5

LIMITED LICENCES – MORETON BAY

Moreton Bay, because it was entirely located within the jurisdiction of Queensland, could be regulated to some extent under the obsolete Fisheries Acts, 1957-62. Although I was unable to directly limit licences, a back door approach was possible by closing an area to all fishing, and then issuing a limited number of permits authorising selected vessels to trawl for prawns during each season.

The Moreton Bay prawn trawling industry was in a mess. Each year there would be complaints of "overfishing", strife between the Bay fleet of small trawlers, which could not fish ocean waters, and some large trawlers from the ocean fishing grounds and a few from interstate which entered the Bay Fishery at times. There were also loud noises from the public about "killing all the juvenile whiting and bream".

It was clear that the small boat fleet alone was as much as the Moreton Bay prawn stocks could sustain, and that the annual influx of large offshore boats needed to be controlled during the time when ocean king prawns were scarce.

I devised a permit scheme giving preference to the trawler owners whose living depended solely on the Moreton Bay prawn stocks, which provided for their future financial wellbeing and for recruitment of newcomers. This Fishery was an important training ground for cadet fishermen, as well as forming a low cost means of entry into the prawning industry.

Permits were to be granted only to holders of Master Fishermen's licences who had fished the Moreton Bay prawn grounds for at least half of the previous season. These permits were personal to the holder and not transferable. The permit holders were entitled to operate any trawler as its Master. The vessels themselves were not controlled.

This system was intended to limit the number of prawn trawlers operating, as far as possible, to those owned by the local fishermen who had developed the Fishery. It maintained an entry path for recruits by employment as deckie-learners, deckhands and trainee masters until vacancies occurred on the permit list. The system also precluded any trading in permits.

At this point I encountered opposition from some of the boat-owning segment of the industry. The entrepreneurs amongst the trawler owners wanted the permits to be attached to the boats instead of to the master fishermen. They also wanted to be able to transfer the permits from boat to boat, making huge profits by buying worn out boats with permits and replacing them with large vessels.

I suffered a bout of pneumonia at this time, in 1970, and, "guess what", when I returned to my office I found that the bureaucrats had rewritten my carefully planned submission and replaced it with their version which attached the permits to the boats and made them transferable.

These changes negated the effects of the permit system by forcing many of the local fishermen out of the industry and replacing them with entrepreneurs. The changes also increased the fishing effort on the prawn stocks and led, years later, to yet another expensive buy-back scheme. Not to mention threats by some fishermen to barricade the Port of Brisbane, and comments from the Trawlermen's Association such as "What shall we do with Harrison"? I was not able to reverse this action when I returned from sick leave.

It was stated, inter alia, in "The Courier-Mail" of 19th July 2009, as follows:

"The licence buy-back was introduced to reduce commercial fishing in the Bay after the expansion of no-fishing "green" zones in March.

Often in fishing licence buy-back schemes, there is a condition of sale that prevents a former licence holder returning to the same fishing area for up to three years. That didn't exist.

But under the Moreton Bay buy-back rules there was nothing to stop those who sold licences from buying a permit in a private sale from local fishermen who retained multiple licences.

The State Government spent $15,100,000 on the buy-back scheme.

A government spokesman hailed the buy-back as a success. He said the target was to buy 94 licences, and in the end 118 licences had been surrendered."

In the original permit scheme created by the bureaucrats in opposition to my advice in 1970, there was no provision in the law to prevent or control multiple ownership of permits by investors. In the 2009 buy-back there was no provision to stop the re-entry of a fisherman who had been bought out through the purchase of one of these multiple permits. The result was that some men doubled their money at the expense of the taxpayer, and the Fishery was still over- crowded.

It is interesting to compare this situation with the taxi industry in which the market value of a licence has become a controlling factor.

CHAPTER 6

FISHERIES ACTS

In 1962, before I took up duty in the Department of Harbours and Marine in February 1963, an attempt to update the Fisheries Acts 1957-62 had been made.

The amendments were concerned with the increase of licence fees and penalties, as well as some new netting regulations mainly concerned with tunnel nets. The Acts did not address fisheries management problems or provide any new powers to enable such management to be introduced. The 1962 amendments demonstrated the absence of any Fisheries Management Skills in Queensland at the time.

Soon after my arrival I found that the Fisheries Acts 1957-62, even as recently amended, were so dated as to be inadequate for their purpose. I was told by my Department Head that it had just been amended and I could not amend it again for a few years. In effect I was told that I would have no legal powers to enable me to carry out my duties.

The Act lacked most of the provisions essential for the management of fishery resources, such as limited licence fisheries and the measurement of catch and effort, particularly when fishing grounds extended into Commonwealth-controlled and International waters. There were no provisions dealing with the processing, carriage and landing of fish and the use of mother ships. The Acts were also silent on matters such as noxious fish and fish farming - only whaling, pearling and oyster farming were covered. Other deficiencies included the lack of a Fisheries Research Trust Fund, provisions covering Fishing Industry representation and organisation, marine parks powers, and many other matters were also absent.

The Fisheries Acts 1957-62 which I had to work with had only rudimentary Regulatory provisions, and the unwieldy Order-in-Council was the only means available to take any action. Timely Regulatory action was not possible.

In situations confined entirely to State waters, it was possible to achieve some useful management measures, such as the limited entry prawn fishery in Moreton Bay (refer to Chapter 5 – Limited Licences-Moreton Bay) and some catch and effort statistics through a log book scheme, both of which I introduced.

In 1968 I commenced the enormous task of drafting an up-to-date Act (much of it being done at home in my own time), and when it was completed I continued my efforts to send it to the Parliamentary Draughtsman for action.

I was prevented by the bureaucracy from proceeding with this for several years, and it was not until after the turmoil of the Gulf prawn problems of 1973 that I was able to move on the part of the Act dealing with Fish Processing. This was enacted in 1974.

Soon afterwards, when the Royal Commission into Oil Drilling on the Great Barrier Reef ended in 1974, I was given the go ahead to take my latest draft of the whole new Fisheries Bill to the Parliamentary Draughtsman.

I had numerous meetings with the Parliamentary Draughtsman and took Noel Haysom, my Assistant, with me on several occasions. I had reached this final stage in drafting the new legislation and had completed the new Bill Book, with the Minister's speech, when I was replaced as Director of Fisheries (refer to Chapter 19 – Demotion).

One of the officers appointed in my place in 1975 withdrew my Fisheries Bill. In 1976 Noel Haysom, then Assistant Executive Officer, was given the priority task by the Director of the Department of Aboriginal and Islanders Advancement, Pat Killoran, of getting the proposed new Fisheries Act ready for presentation to Parliament. Fortunately my Bill book had not been destroyed. The Bill needed amendment to incorporate Marine National Parks which had been added to Fisheries responsibilities. (A Bill Book is the copy of a proposed Act of Parliament presented to the House by the Minister for debate, together with his second reading speech).

Thus, two more years were lost before Fisheries Management became possible in Queensland. By then I was no longer in charge of Fisheries.

Fishing is the last true "hunting" activity. Fishing is not comparable with farming or husbandry. Fish stocks are wild resources which have no owner, except perhaps the Coastal State, until they are captured.

The Fisheries Manager has the task of sharing the fish resources equitably between the participants so that the sustainable yield is not exceeded. The tools by which this management can be achieved are the powers provided by up-to-date Fisheries Laws. Furthermore, these Laws have to be identical to, or compatible with Commonwealth Laws, and the Laws of all the other States which may share the resources. This was very difficult to achieve and was the reason behind my recommendation to set up the Northern Fisheries Research Committee as a negotiating forum.

In October 1981, Mr. Dale Brian, Chairman of the Queensland Commercial Fishermen's Organisation (Australian Fisheries), said "Queensland has in the main been a disaster for the industry, primarily because there is not, and never has been, any master plan, and any attempts at management in the past have proved to be too little and too late."

To this statement I can only reply:

"The tools of the Fisheries Manager are the Fisheries Laws";

"No Legislation - No Management";

"Obsolete Laws Strangle Progress".

CHAPTER 7

CROWN of THORNS STARFISH

The second of my problem files, awaiting my arrival in Queensland, referred to the destruction of coral by the Crown of Thorns Starfish. I decided to ask Noel Haysom to visit Green Island and to report on the situation.

The Crown of Thorns Starfish was a comparatively unknown organism, quite rare, but well distributed through the Great Barrier Reef. At first I suspected it was, like other starfish and echinoderms, subject to rare and unexplained population explosions, but the literature suggested that no such population explosions of Crown of Thorns Starfish (Acanthaster planci) had been recorded anywhere in the world, with the possible exception of the Red Sea during the Roman Empire era. When Noel Haysom's preliminary report arrived I became concerned at the extent of the damage being caused to the living coral.

During an earlier brief visit to Green Island I had been appalled by the state of the reef flat. The then tourist operator daily transported some 300 visitors to the Island for lunch and a walk on the Reef. In consequence the reef flat around the resort was almost barren, having been trampled to death. Waste materials were also dumped off the reef edge contributing an undesirable nutrient load on the system. The fact that the Crown of Thorns was first reported as a problem at Green Island made me suspicious.

For all of the above reasons I formed the tentative opinion that the Crown of Thorns Starfish phenomenon was in some way caused by man's activities.

The Great Barrier Reef is the world's largest assemblage of living coral. It is the responsibility of the State of Queensland to look after it, and the buck appeared to stop with me once more.

I had decided that it was essential to discover what had caused this problem, which appeared to be getting worse all the time.

If the population explosion were a natural or cyclical phenomenon we would have to live with it. If it was a man-made problem it must be addressed. It was also necessary to protect, as far as possible, reef areas used by the tourist industry. I recommended to the Government that funds be provided to employ a Research Officer and two technical assistants to commence a survey, and a research programme, to find out as much as possible about this phenomenon, particularly the areas affected, rate of spread and some basic knowledge of the life cycle of this animal.

The tourist resort operators were very concerned and were exerting considerable pressure on the Government. This, no doubt, assisted me in winning approval for funds for my initial research programme. No funds were approved by the Government for population control. Some resort operators employed divers to kill rhe starfish on nearby reefs.

When the funds were approved I recruited Bob Pearson, a Marine Biologist, with some experience of Coral Reef work and two technical assistants. I also purchased a suitable vessel and equipment, had the officers trained in scuba diving by the Queensland Water Police, and transferred them to accommodation I had arranged on Green Island.

Meanwhile, I consulted Professor W. Stephenson (Professor of Zoology at the University of Queensland), and was able to arrange with him for Dr. Robert Endean (a Reader in his Department) to assist Bob Pearson in planning his programme and to supervise the fieldwork on a part-time basis. Dr. Endean was an internationally respected Scientist, specialising in marine toxicology in the coral reef environment. He had wide coral reef experience and was already familiar with Acanthaster planci. Furthermore, Bob Pearson had been one of his students at the University of Queensland.

The first reports from this study included a number of recommendations and findings, some of which were that:

1. Six coral reefs in the Cairns to Innisfail area were under attack by the starfish, including Green Island;
2. The starfish breeding season was restricted to December/January, and each adult starfish was capable of producing millions of eggs;
3. While feeding on plankton, the larvae drifted freely for about three weeks before settling to the sea bed.

Possible causes of the population explosion included:

1. The release of predator pressure on the adult starfish by the removal of large numbers of triton shells by shell collectors (the only predator of adult starfish then known);
2. Pollution by run-off carrying pesticides or nutrients from cane farms;
3. Dredging or other destructive activities.

Dr. Endean suggested the triton shellfish, at the time the only known predator of the adult Crown of Thorns Starfish, had been over-collected from the central reef area by the trochus fishermen. A large fleet of pearling luggers, based on Thursday Island, fished the Great Barrier Reef waters each year for trochus shells to supply the pearl button trade, until the late 1950s. The divers had a free day when they ended each trip, which they used to collect shells to sell to collectors. The triton or giant trumpet shell was quite valuable and prized. There were large numbers of triton shells stored for sale in tea chests on Palm Island off Townsville over a long period of time.

Reports from other parts of the Pacific and from Japan and America suggested outbreaks of starfish were occurring near centres of human population, and not in remote areas. On air trips in North Queensland I had observed that plumes of silt-laden water from the rivers extended for many miles out into the Coral Sea during the wet season.

Whilst working in Ghana, West Africa, in the 1950s I had been involved in work to extend the effective range of insecticides in rivers to control the filter feeding larvae of the black fly (Simulium damnosum). We found that, when attached to very finely divided clay particles, the lethal effects of the DDT on the larvae were extended for many miles down the rivers. The clay particles acted as a carrier and were not diluted like a solute (dissolved substance). Furthermore, the effects on fish were much less than those of DDT in solution.

River banks in the tropics are mainly mangrove covered, usually cleared by the cane farmers who farm right to the water's edge. In 1967 I presented a paper to the Australian Conservation foundation "Caring for Queensland" showing the value and importance of mangroves (refer to Chapter 9 – Mangroves, Deception Bay Laboratory). I wanted mangroves to be preserved to serve as a filter. I created the first Fisheries Habitat Reserves in Queensland, in Moreton Bay, in January 1969.

It occurred to me that the silt that I observed in the Coral Sea might be carrying pollutants or nutrients from the cane farms and affecting the survival of starfish larvae, enabling many more to settle on the reefs. This process would be assisted by the bare patches of reef where tourist traffic had killed the coral which is itself a predator on the larvae.

In passing the 1968 report by Bob Pearson and Dr. Endean to the Government, I recommended that more time was needed to determine the cause of the problem, which I suspected was man-made. The Government agreed to extend the research programme, but refused to supply the funds for starfish control measures at the tourist resorts.

During the second year of research the starfish had spread to about one-third of the platform reefs within the reef lagoon between Cairns and Townsville, and were now uncontrollable except in localised areas such as tourist resorts. The infested reefs were too numerous and widespread as well as being more distant from shore.

In 1969, Dr. Endean and I were invited to Guam to advise an international team of marine scientists on the starfish problem. The team had been recruited to survey reefs throughout the American Pacific area by the American Government. While in Guam we were able to see the extensive damage to the local reefs. The report which had been suppressed by the Queensland Government was used by Dr. Endean in this briefing and became public knowledge.

Dr. Endean and I were next invited to visit Japan to view an experiment to create an electric barrier to contain the starfish. Professor Suehiro (tutor in marine biology to His Majesty Hirohito, Emperor of Japan) had set up an experiment using copper wires and a car battery which caused the starfish to move away from one wire. I pointed out that ions of copper released into the water by electrolysis might be the causative factor, not the electric field. I suggested a further trial using stainless steel or carbon electrodes instead of copper. This would test the efficacy of an electric field. Copper is very toxic in the marine environment.

We were then asked to attend the Imperial Palace to talk to His Royal Highness Akihito the Crown Prince (now The Reigning Emperor), who is a qualified Biologist, about the starfish problem. We enjoyed a cup of tea and a pleasant hour of conversation during which we showed some slides.

It was reported in "The Australian" on 7th March 1971, "The Queensland Government has suppressed three vital reports by its own experts on devastation of the Great Barrier Reef by the Crown of Thorns Starfish." Indeed Premier Bjelke-Petersen had ordered the Pearson/Endean Report be stamped confidential and not to be released.

While this research was continuing Premier Bjelke-Petersen, announced:

> "The Crown of Thorns is not destroying the Reef - I am quite clear in my own mind that there is no real cause for concern, and recent publicity has presented an alarming picture of the situation. There is no vast plague destroying the Reef."
>
> (Source: "Requiem For The Reef" - Peter James 1976).

The use of a glass bottomed boat gave me a reasonable picture of the situation coupled with talking to Bob Pearson after some of his dives. I then had the opportunity to join a Japanese expedition for three weeks and to make numerous dives in a miniature submarine. This was a wartime mini submarine, like those used in the Sydney Harbour attack, which had been converted. Visibility through the tiny portholes was restricted but I gained some useful information. I had some difficulty squeezing my large frame through the conning tower and over the battery casing, but did not actually get stuck.

We found no evidence of adult starfish migration in deeper waters between the reefs or on the reef slopes. The submarine was able to dive to the sea floor between the reefs where our divers could not go. This supported the idea that the animals were moving from reef to reef as drifting larvae, and not as adults on the sea floor.

Geoffrey Harrison on the submarine.

The Crown of Thorns Starfish had now become highly controversial. The media were having a field day, and the work done by Dr. Robert Endean and Bob Pearson was being questioned by the Premier, who set up a joint Federal/State Government Committee of Enquiry in 1970 to enquire into the problem. None of its members had any expertise in coral reef ecology, or the Crown of Thorns Starfish.

The Committee of Enquiry set up by the Premier to confirm his views was chaired by an eminent Human Geneticist. The Secretary, C.Lloyd Harris (known as Lloyd Harris), was Chief Administration Officer in the Department of Primary Industries, with whom I had often disagreed on Fisheries matters. He was the author of this Committee's report. Other members included a Professor of Geology (I understand that later he had connections with the oil industry); a senior Scientist from CSIRO who was a

Planktologist with little experience in a coral environment; the Professor of Zoology of Queensland University, primarily an ichthyologist, with expertise in Moreton Bay, and with little coral reef experience; and the Director-General of the Department of Primary Industries, a biochemist.

According to one researcher who had been involved with the reef studies, the list of members read more like the Mad Hatter's Tea Party than an official Committee on the Starfish problem.

The 1970 Committee of Enquiry moved on to my views about causes:

> "Harrison was quite definite that he considered the plagues a result of man's interference, although this could have been by any number of means; shell gathering, pollution, dredging, or a combination of several" (Source: "Requiem For The Reef" by Peter James, 1976).

When I was removed from the position of controlling Fisheries research, no further work was done to determine the cause of the Crown of Thorns Starfish plague. The Premier's view, that it was only a passing natural occurrence, prevailed. Dr. Endean expressed his concern on television and in the press and I supported him. We predicted that the starfish numbers would die back after eating most of the coral on the central reef platforms, and return when some coral had regenerated. This is exactly what has happened. The starfish have returned three times.

I will not write in detail on this committee's report, which can be found in the literature. I will quote only some extracts from the recorded evidence and the Committee's conclusions, which diverge greatly.

Regarding the Summary of Evidence given at the 1970 Committee of Enquiry into the Crown of Thorns Starfish problem, as recorded in "Requiem For The Reef" by Peter James in 1976, only three witnesses subscribed to the view that the plague was man-made, and they were Dr. Robert Endean, Geoffrey Harrison and Dr. Richard Chesher.

Dr. Chesher was an American Marine Biologist and a consultant to the USA Government on reef problems whom Dr. Endean and I met in Guam. All three of us considered the plague serious and man-made, i.e. through tritons, pollution and/or dredging, and that coral regeneration would be very slow.

Bob Pearson was another Queensland witness and a Marine Biologist with several years' fieldwork and research. He considered the plague was serious with variable causes such as predators, tritons, shrimps, etc., and that coral regeneration would be very slow.

Noel Haysom, my Assistant Biologist, another Queensland witness, held the indecisive view that the plague was "? Serious," and, based on recent research supervising, Mr. Haysom held no views in regard to causes of the starfish problem or the rate of coral regeneration.

Ernest Grant, Marine Biologist and another Queensland witness, held the view that the plague was natural, that coral regeneration was rapid, and that the cause was cyclic, which views were based on no research. He did not have any involvement in the research program, but was my senior staff member.

The Committee dismissed pollution as a cause because no traces of pesticides were found in the bodies of starfish. It failed to consider enhanced larval survival due to nutrients carried by silt from cane farms increasing their food supply in the low nutrient waters of the Coral Sea.

The Committee recommended that a continuing research program should be set up, which was to be controlled by a new Committee. This Body comprised Noel Haysom and the Chief Administration officer of the Department of Primary Industries Lloyd Harris. This new Committee effectively separated Dr. Endean and me from any starfish activities in the future, and allocated no funds to research concerning the causes of the problem.

Regarding the report of the 1970 Committee of Enquiry, Premier Joh Bjelke-Petersen said:

"The report clearly vindicates the stand taken by the Queensland Government. It must raise serious doubts as to the competence of those who sought to spread gloom" (Source: "Requiem For The Reef by Peter James, 1976").

In an interview on the ABC "7:30 Report" in 1988 (almost a year after exiting politics) Sir Joh Bjelke-Petersen said:

"Hundreds of people went up there with spears. It was like a plague of mice, catching mice with a lone mouse trap, setting mice traps all around. We couldn't keep up with the supply of hundreds of thousands of dollars he (he meant me) kept demanding, all the time, to live up there having a mighty good time as it were."

In the recommendations which formed a part of my first report to the Government on the starfish problem, I pointed out that, since only six reefs adjacent to Green Island were affected, it would be possible for divers to reduce the population of starfish so as to slow down their further spread to more distant reefs. I recommended a sum of around $120,000 be made available for this purpose. By the time my report had been released by Premier Bjelke-Petersen, the starfish had already spread and this opportunity had been lost. Control by divers was no longer possible, except on reefs attached to tourist resort islands.

The Premier took his advice from politicised bureaucrats and experts in fields other than coral or marine ecology. He never sought advice directly from me, his Chief Fisheries adviser, unlike the previous Premiers Frank Nicklin and Jack Pizzey.

For example, as recorded in "Requiem For The Reef":

"Premier Bjelke-Petersen and the Deputy Premier held an hour long interview with Mr. Ben Cropp, a well known diver and spear-fisherman who had made an underwater film on the Reef. Why Mr. Cropp was chosen to be interviewed is open to speculation. Before the interview, Mr. Cropp's had been one of the lone voices raised against what might be termed the Endeanview. Back in May of that year he had referred to "a so-called plague," adding: 'The starfish is probably helping rather than hindering the growth of corals. We are coming to the conclusion that it is not a plague and that starfish wander in packs and play an important part in the natural growth of the reef.' Mr. Cropp did not enlighten reporters as to whom the 'we' might be, nor did he state the basis for his hypothesis that starfish wandered in packs, since it had never been recorded before the present infestations. Further, by his own admission, he spent most of his time at the southern end of the Barrier Reef, outside the areas of infestation. He had not visited any of those infested, except Green Island, where his contact with the animal included the placing of one on a plate coral to photograph. Nonetheless, he stated he was quite confident that the starfish was merely hastening the growth of corals by eating away the veneer of live growth (in much the same way, perhaps, that locust plagues hasten the growth of grasses and shrubs and crops?). After being eaten away, he added, the dead coral collapsed to form a strong platform on which the new coral grew."

On the 15th July 1987 in "The Courier-Mail" a letter was published (Letters to the Editor). Extracts from this letter are as follows:

"For many years now there have been two conflicting views as to the seriousness of the damage inflicted by the Crown of Thorns Starfish on the Coral of the Great Barrier Reef.

One school of thought (and one I agree with) is that led by Dr. Endean of Queensland University, who argues that the damage is very serious indeed and that the Government should have taken direct positive action to reduce the starfish population years ago.

But the other view is that (obviously) taken by the Government advisers, namely that, although the damage caused is regrettable, it is nevertheless a natural phenomenon and therefore human intervention is not welcome" (Name and address supplied).

I chose to reply to this letter and my reply was published in "The Courier Mail" on 17th July 1987 (Letters to the Editor). Extracts from this letter follow:

"I am in full agreement with the letter from (name supplied) regarding the serious and continuing damage to our Great Barrier Reef by the Crown of Thorns Starfish.

I must, however, take issue with the writer in regard to the Government's advisers, all of whom were not supportive of the "whitewash view".

As Chief Adviser to the Government on Fisheries from 1963, I set up a research project on the Crown of Thorns Starfish with Dr. R. Endean as co-ordinator. His 1968 report emphasised the damage being done to the Reef. I concurred with his findings and maintained that control was possible at that time when only about six reefs were infested.

This report was shelved (and stamped confidential by the Government) for more than a year until my efforts and public statements by Dr. Endean forced its publication in 1969. No action was taken by the Government on the report."

As I have already stated in this chapter my advice on this matter was ignored by the Government in favour of the non-professional advice of certain bureaucrats and advisers such as Ben Cropp. The consequent delay had rendered any attempt at control of starfish numbers impossible.

Running an almost parallel course with the Crown of Thorns affair was the controversy over oil drilling on the Reef. Premier Bjelke-Petersen, said on 14th January 1970, "I am convinced that drilling in Repulse Bay should go ahead and that it is quite safe. An expert survey has already been completed in a most competent way."

Fortunately, the decision on drilling the Reef was temporarily taken out of the politicians' hands. The JAPEX well was delayed owing to industrial troubles on the rig fabrication site in America. The Company then offered 5,000 dollars towards conducting an enquiry into Oil Drilling on the Reef, and a Royal Commission was later set up – against the protestations of the Premier of Queensland, Joh Bjelke-Petersen. Not that a Royal Commission would necessarily be a concern for him, as he stated at the outset: "The Royal Commission will serve no purpose" And "Queensland will not necessarily be bound by the findings of the Commission" (Source: Requiem For The Reef" – Peter James, 1976).

The Royal Commission was held between 1970 and 1974.

An article in 'The Courier-Mail' on the 1st January 2011 under the heading **"Joh against protecting Barrier Reef"** by Jessica Marszalek said:

"The Joh Bjelke-Petersen government furiously opposed the World Heritage declaration of the Great Barrier Reef 30 years ago, arguing only sections of it should be protected.

Recently released Cabinet documents from 1980 show the coalition government was dead against the Reef's listing ... which happened the following year.

Current Queensland Public Works Minister Robert Schwarten, who has released the Cabinet documents, said the Bjelke-Petersen government's intention had been to do exploratory mining on the reef for oil.

Originally raised in January 1978, the idea to list the Reef was set to be debated by the Australian Heritage Commission in February, 1980.

A month before that, Cabinet resolved to send a letter to the commission reaffirming the Queensland government's objection to that.

It said the Great Barrier Reef Marine Park Authority already existed to assess the "conservation, management and economic potential" of the area.

"By examining the Great Barrier Reef region by region, the authority has acknowledged that there are areas of differing conservation potential," the letter said.

"... it would be appropriate, therefore, to list only areas of prime ecological significance on the register as they are assessed and identified by the Great Barrier Reef Marine Park Authority."

Mr. Schwarten said it was interesting to compare the environmently aware world of 2010 to 1980, when the environmental debate began in Queensland.

"The environment was foremost on everybody's lips but for the wrong reason," he said.

"... ironically, one of the sticking points was that the Queensland government was demanding payment for the mining rights from the Reef east of Cairns."

"Can you imagine anybody suggesting today that we mine on the Great Barrier Reef or that the Queensland government is looking for compensation to not mine on it?"

The Great Barrier Reef is the world's largest World Heritage Area and is the world's most extensive coral reef system, celebrated for its rich biological diversity. "

It was stated in the "Melbourne Age" of 27th November 1985, by Greg Borschmann and John Larkin re "Whitewash Claim on Starfish", inter alia:

"The tourism operators feared the publicity that the reef was dead; that people would stop coming. I think they and the sugar cane farmers are the lobbies which pressured the Government. Earlier this month came some vindication of the "Endean-Harrison line." The House of Representative Standing Committee on Environment and Conservation said "It is reasonable to conclude that the starfish outbreaks may not be entirely natural but may be influenced by the widespread human activity."

It was reported in "The Courier-Mail" on 31st January 2003, inter alia, (Editorial) –

"Land-based pollution is threatening the future of the Great Barrier Reef." According to a report prepared by nine scientists and published this week, "there is a serious risk to the long term sustainable functioning of at least the in-shore reef areas and........action is necessary to avoid...........long term adverse impact." "The problem could extend to off-shore reefs as well."

Christine Flatley in "The Courier Mail" reported on 23rd February 2007:

Run-off reaches coral - action to save reef

PESTICIDE run-off may be polluting larger areas of the Great Barrier Reef than originally thought.

A series of satellite images obtained by CSIRO scientists have confirmed for the first time that sediment plumes travel to the outer reef and beyond.

It was originally believed the plumes – which can contain pesticides, herbicides and other micro pollutants from river systems – affected only the inner Great Barrier Reef lagoon and the inner reef corals.

But the new images, taken by NASA'S MODIS satellite by GeoScience Australia's Alice Springs site between February 9 and 13 show they are travelling up to 135km offshore.

The images were taken during the heavy rains in far north Queensland, and show floodwaters carrying a larger sediment load than during regular rainfall and river flow.

CSIRO scientist Arnold Dekker said the images would change the way scientists analysed reef pollution and that they showed land care practices needed to be improved to save the Reef from destruction.

"This is the first time it's been really proven that this is a phenomenon that we need to start incorporating into our studies of how we manage the land and what flows from the land, and how it affects the Reef," he said.

"It's a good example of nature being a bit more complex than we think (and) we have to start studying how often these sediments and contaminants reach the outer reefs."

The Great Barrier Reef Marine Park Authority is overseeing the implementation of the 10-year $40 million Reef Water Quality Protection Plan to improve land management practices in the catchment area.

It's a plan that Dr. Dekker believes should be supported by farmers, tourism authorities and the government.

He said revegetating areas around waterways would help catch the sediments before they reached the ocean.

(Refer to earlier pages in Chapter 7 regarding the black fly - Simulium Damnosum from my work in Ghana in the 1950s).

The Swain's reef complex at the southern end of the Great Barrier Reef is a vast uncharted maze of reefs and channels. When I visited the area in 1967 it was navigable only by local knowledge in reasonable weather. The visit was intended to discover if the Crown of Thorns Starfish had reached as far south. Unfortunately part way through our trip a cyclone moved in stranding us for days. Luckily our pilot found shelter from the very rough seas in a lagoon. The howling winds, which occurred and reversed as the cyclonic eye passed over us, caused our anchor to drag repeatedly. It was a rough experience and I was pleased to get back to Yeppoon, after being out of communication for about two days.

My younger daughter Celia Mary, then 14 years, wrote a poem in 1980 for a school project. This was many years before it was officially accepted in 2003 that the Crown of Thorns Starfish problem was man-made, caused by pollution (nutrients carried by run-off from the cane farms).

I enjoyed the poem and I reproduce it in full on the following pages.

CROWN OF THORNS

The Coral slowly dies,
Who cares?
"Our" reef is dying,
But it is not "my" problem,
Is it yours?

I don't have to live there
in that death trap,
where the Crown of Thorns
are killing all coral in their path.
Soon sea life in the area will slowly fade
And die.

I suppose "I" could write letters
Complaining about the spread
Of these thorns,
For what they are doing to "our"
Queensland's main tourist attraction.

Yes, Tourist attraction,
Ah! That made you take notice, didn't it?

Sydney has the Opera House,
Canberra has the Jet,
Northern Territory, well, she has
Ayers Rock and buffalo.
Tasmania, her apples.
And us –

Soon we'll have nothing.

Then what will happen ?

Yes: No tourist attraction.
Fingers will point at what used to be
Queensland's star attraction
The all beautiful Great Barrier Reef.
Heron Island,
She's still waiting in line
for this gruesome animal,
waiting to be pounced on
while not looking.These prickly monsters,
Where did they come from?
"I know", there have been a few there all the time;
But this extraordinary number of Killing creatures, now,
Is uncountable

Why did they come?
Many think numbers increased
Because of man's – yes, you and I –
Our interference with our Reef's natural Form,

When will they go?
When they have devoured all the coral?
Then they'll move on, and ,
And hopefully most will die.

And what of our golden heritage for future generations?

Well who is to blame?
"Us", our interference:

"Man".

Celia Mary Harrison, 1980

CHAPTER 8

MARCO POLO

As the Head of Queensland Fisheries I was invited to membership of the Great Barrier Reef Committee, an international scientific committee set up to study the Reef following the first Coral Reef Symposium in the 1950s. Later, after I had become a member as a Scientist in my own right, I served as Vice-President for a term. I then had access to the files and the history of the Heron Island Research Station, which was operated jointly by the Great Barrier Reef Committee and the University of Queensland.

These files also detailed the sorry tale of a breakdown in the relations between the Heron Island Research Station staff and the Poulsen family, who owned and operated the tourist resort on Heron Island. This explained a lot to me about my appointment to take charge of Fisheries in Queensland, but which I will not enlarge upon here.

The Committee was asked to organise a second Coral Reef Symposium, and it was soon discovered that some 370 Scientists from all over the world wished to attend a ten day meeting. In the 1970s such a large group could not be accommodated in Queensland anywhere north of Brisbane, and a lack of local charter vessels prevented visits to the Great Barrier Reef.

As a member of the executive committee, I suggested an approach to the Shipping Company, P&O, to charter a cruise ship which could visit the Reef as far north as Lizard Island, as well as providing space for the scientific meetings and living accommodation. My suggestion was accepted, and the "Marco Polo" a ship able to carry about 400 passengers was chartered. I give much credit to Dr. Patricia Mather of the University of Queensland, as the chief organiser of this huge undertaking. The Symposium was successful. The ship sailed from Brisbane to Lizard Island, and visited numerous reefs for diving on the way south to Heron Island. Three series of seminars were run daily and the proceedings were published later in two large volumes. The expedition made a profit which financed a small bursary.

The only thing that did not go as planned was that the Premier of Queensland, Joh Bjelke-Petersen, refused permission for me to attend the Symposium.

Even when the Vice-Chancellor of Queensland University, Sir Zelman Cowen, (later the Governor General) telephoned the Premier and expressed a wish that I attend, I was still not allowed to go.

On one occasion I was awaiting the arrival of my Minister, the Hon. Vic Sullivan, outside Parliament House when the Premier came out. He spoke to me about the birds in the trees and I took the opportunity to speak about the Crown of Thorns Starfish. He then recognised me and immediately turned his back and moved away.

Two members of my staff were allowed to attend the Symposium and their expenses were paid by the Queensland Government. My wife and I attended the send-off party on board, and we waved our goodbyes from the wharf. It was VERY EMBARRASSING. Sundry questions were asked about my absence from the trip.

At the end of the voyage I received a chart of the voyage signed by all the scientists on board, which I still value.

MANGROVES, DECEPTION BAY LABORATORY

The Gulf Prawn Survey ended in the late 1960s, and Dr. Kesteven, CSIRO, and I considered that the research team should be kept together and transferred to the East Coast to continue its prawn studies in the East Coast fishery, where this work was sorely needed. I submitted this proposal to the Queensland Government and received approval, provided the CSIRO staff (the majority) remained in the team. I rented temporary accommodation in the Redcliffe area and the research team continued its studies from that centre.

Dr. Geoff Kesteven and I also developed a proposal to construct a new laboratory in the Moreton Bay area to provide permanent accommodation for the prawn research team. This proposal, though approved in principle, led to heated discussions between me and my Head of Department in Harbours and Marine, and the Under-Treasurer, over its construction cost and starting date. These financial problems were resolved only after Fisheries was transferred to the Department of Primary Industries in 1969/1970.

The Department of Primary Industries, being a science based Department, was able to provide the capital sum required for an adequate laboratory, and large tanks and pumping system to supply experimental aquaria with filtered water.

For once a project of mine was not blocked as it was in the Department of Harbours and Marine. However, when the Deception Bay Laboratory was finally opened in 1970, I was not included in the opening ceremony.

The building had been paid for by the Queensland Department of Primary Industries. The laboratory apparatus and most of the staff were provided by the CSIRO.

Thus, the first Queensland Fisheries Laboratory came into being providing, for the first time, a base for State officers to conduct fisheries research.

The CSIRO built its own laboratory at Cleveland some years later and transferred its staff there. By which time, under the Department of Primary Industries umbrella, and thanks to its scientist Head, the Director-General, Dr. J. R. Harvey, I had been able to build up a small team of fisheries scientists, and Queensland had its own working research facility.

Queensland's first fisheries laboratory.

Laboratory opening.

Whilst in the planning stage of the laboratory, I was involved in the search for a suitable site. It had to be Crown land in/or adjacent to mangroves with access to clean sea and fresh water. A site at Deception Bay was eventually located. The search for land made me aware, for the first time, of the extent of coastal reclamation for housing development, and the very high rate of conversion of mangrove land into dollars through the construction of canal estates. This alarmed me and I initiated a brief survey of the remaining mangrove areas owned by the Crown from Caloundra to the Gold Coast.

The mangrove areas, together with adjacent marine grass beds, are vitally important to the preservation of the coastal fish stocks. These zones exhibit an extremely high productivity of fish food at the lowest trophic level. Sunlight in the eel grass areas, organisms breaking down mangrove leaf litter, and mud eating animals generate most of the food supply for the coastal fish stocks. These areas also provide shelter for juvenile marine species.

Mangrove swamps, both coastal and riverine, provide a filter mechanism which traps much of the sediments and pollutants carried off the land by the rain before they reach the sea, thus purifying the water and reducing erosion by trapping the sediments.

In 1968/1969 I drafted Orders in Council reserving the most important of the remaining mangrove areas in Moreton Bay, and protecting them from development. I called these areas Habitat Reserves, since their purpose was to protect the habitat as a fish food-producing engine, whilst not preventing normal fishing activities. I sited the first Fisheries Habitat Reserves in Moreton Bay in January 1969. The Fisheries Acts, 1957-62, contained very weak provisions for the creation of Reserves, which I was later able to strengthen when I drafted a new Act in the 1970s, but my Habitat Reserves served their purpose, and I extended the survey northwards as far as Cairns and progressively added more Habitat Reserves as time went on.

The old reserves, which already existed when I came to Queensland, were protective of juvenile fish and so called nursery areas. They banned all fishing activities within their waters. They really did not serve much purpose.

As a part of my campaign to establish this mangrove protection, I presented a paper at a Symposium "Caring for Queensland", organised by The Australian Conservation Foundation, held at The University of Queensland, St. Lucia, Brisbane, on 14-15 October 1967. This Paper was subsequently updated, and a Bibliography added before being submitted to the Royal Commission into Oil Drilling on the Great Barrier Reef 1970-74.

I believe that my introduction of Habitat Reserves was the first serious attempt in Australia to preserve the basic food chain of the coastal fish stocks, as opposed to banning all fishing activities in an area. After the Moreton Bay Habitat Reserves were declared, I was able to have an officer transferred to the Branch to locate and survey other important mangrove areas to the north, and to extend Habitat Reserves as far as Cairns. A paper was published by "Fisheries Queensland" a service of the Department of Employment, Economic Development and Innovation in November 2011 with the headline "Frank Olson – founding father of Queensland's declared Fish Habitat Area Network", made no reference to my paper of 14-15 October 1967, "Caring for Queensland". I delegated this survey work to Frank Olsen. I congratulate him for the way in which he fulfilled my concept "Caring for Queensland" (preservation of mangroves). I must remind him and Fisheries Queensland that I coined the phrase "Habitat Reserves" in October 1967, and they were not in use under the 1957 Fisheries Act when Fisheries Nurseries existed.

CHAPTER 10

FISHERIES OFFICERS' CONFERENCE

The third urgent file saved up for me to deal with when I arrived in Queensland in 1963 concerned the next meeting scheduled of the Australian Fisheries Officers' Conference, (which later evolved into the Standing Committee on Fisheries).

This comprised a three day meeting of the chief officers of Fisheries from all the States and Territories, Papua New Guinea, the Commonwealth and the CSIRO, followed by a one day meeting of the Australian Fisheries Council comprising all the Commonwealth and State Fisheries Ministers. This meeting was only a few months ahead, and I would have to speak for Queensland on numerous agenda items and brief my Minister (Sir Thomas Hiley) for the Council meeting. I had a lot to learn in a short time. I also had to prepare a paper on each agenda item for the meeting on subjects and issues quite new to me.

This meeting took place in Melbourne and I was helped a lot by Cedric Setter, Assistant Secretary in charge of Fisheries in

Canberra, who became a friend in need. The meetings were useful because I was able to get to know my colleagues around Australia, as well as some of their problems. It was also an opportunity to meet my Minister and to work with him for several hours. This won for me the valuable gift of access to Sir Thomas Hiley without going through the bureaucrats. Unfortunately, he retired for health reasons not long afterwards and this left me blocked again.

The next Fisheries Officers' Conference was scheduled to take place in Queensland, over a year later. I became the Chairman and host and I had time to prepare. This time it was not all new ground. I received little help from my staff on the agenda items and had to rely on the files for information. However, I was fortunate in having an officer on my staff who normally supervised the shark meshing contracts. He was a very good organiser and took care of booking accommodation, transport from the airport and other details. His name was Treasure Jones, and he was a real treasure.

Since I was the Chairman I arranged for my most senior officer, the Marine Biologist on my staff, Ernest Grant, to take the Queensland seat at the conference. I briefed him on the various agenda items so that he could speak for Queensland. On the first day of the conference his seat was vacant. He reported sick for the whole meeting. I was left to manage both the Chair and the State representation. It was a difficult and embarrassing situation.

After the meeting finished, Minister Hiley had invited all the Commonwealth and State Ministers and State Directors to Heron Island for a fishing weekend. This meant lots more work for me and my organiser, Treasure Jones, but all went well. The Queensland Government paid transport and boat charter costs and the guests paid for their accommodation.

Reading the agenda at the Fisheries Council Meeting in Brisbane.
Sir Thomas Hiley on right.

The Standing Committee on Fisheries set up numerous sub-committees to deal with individual problems. I became a member and served as Chairman of the Education Committee for many years, which organised and ran training courses for Fisheries Officers every third year, and a major Fishing Industry Symposium.

On 6th April 1981, Professor Willett, Vice-Chancellor of Griffith University, Brisbane, was quoted in an article in "The Courier-Mail" suggesting that a School of Fisheries should be established. My long-standing interest in Fisheries Education dating back to my Ghana days persuaded me to write a lengthy submission to Professor Willett. This was followed by a meeting with the Professor in which he underlined the difficulty of establishing a case for a Fisheries School in Brisbane rather than on some southern campus. I wrote making some suggestions which I felt to be helpful in establishing a case.

During the last year of my service in Ghana I had spent about a week in the Fisheries Office of the Food and Agriculture Organisation of the United Nations, in Rome, drafting a plan for a Fisheries School to be established jointly by the FAO and the Government of Ghana under the United Nations Special Fund. I believe the School was established after I had retired from West Africa.

When the Gulf prawn fisheries were building up, I proposed that a new committee be set up called The Northern Fisheries Research Committee, as already stated in Chapter 4 on the Gulf of Carpentaria Prawn Survey. This was approved by the Fisheries Officers' Conference, and then by the Ministers' Council, and became responsible for the co-ordination of Fisheries research and management in northern waters from Broome in Western Australia to Bowen in Queensland, including the Gulf of Carpentaria, the Torres Strait and Papua New Guinea.

This Committee kept me quite busy at times. The members were at State Director level so I could not delegate this work. Later, after I had been replaced as Director, in 1975, a meeting of the Northern Fisheries Research Committee was held. The new administration sent a junior scientific officer to represent Queensland instead of the newly appointed Director of Fisheries, Norm Hall. I was ignored, although available. I received a telephone call from Canberra asking "What is going on?"

The Committee dealing with imported and noxious fish also took much of my time, while I was still the Director of Fisheries, until I delegated this committee work to Noel Haysom.

As usual I had no power under our obsolete Fisheries Acts to control the definition, possession or release of noxious or imported fish. This Committee tried to use Commonwealth Health or Import powers to control the situation. The Customs Department called it a Health problem and the Health Department were equally adamant that it was a matter for Customs. Nothing was done until Queensland's legislation was eventually updated after I had been removed from the scene.

Imported aquarium fish, often from Africa, came in bags of non-sterile water containing water weeds. These often contained snails which could be hosts to various nasty tropical diseases such as Bilharzia. The risks arising from these uncontrolled imports were real and included health as well as fisheries problems. I predicted that Tilapia species, particularly the mouth breeders, were the main threat and, inevitably, would spread in our tropical rivers. I said that they would take over from our indigenous species, just as the European Carp had already damaged many rivers and their fish stocks in the southern States.

The simple solution to this problem would have been Queensland Government legislation to prohibit the possession or release of fish species declared as noxious. I had drafted such legislation in the late 1960s, but the Department Head, Harbours and Marine, said he did not have time to deal with fisheries legislation, and I must manage without it.

Structurally, Australian Fisheries Administration was very complex. Most problems involved several jurisdictions. These could not be fully resolved until the new legislation, which I had drafted years before, came into effect, after I had been removed from my position as Director of Fisheries.

CHAPTER 11

FISH BOARD

My wife and I called at Queensland House in London in 1961 when I was seeking information on Fisheries in Queensland. The only information they could produce was some old Annual Reports from The Fish Board.

Later, after I had been appointed as Chief Inspector of Fisheries and Senior Biologist I visited the Fish Board premises in Brisbane, and all of its branches throughout the State. I found a standard auction marketing system selling the catches of artisanal net fishermen, a new and developing prawn processing operation (in Brisbane), and a mackerel marketing scheme which was guaranteed to fill the freezers with poor quality fish.

I wrote a report making some suggestions and was told, bluntly, to keep my nose out of the Fish Board. It seemed that, although I was appointed to take charge of Fisheries in Queensland, I was to have control over only half the industry.

Briefly, the Fish Board was losing money and the corrective measures that had been taken were ill-advised. Originally the Fish

Board was set up to provide for local marketing of fresh fish, and to do this mainly through an auction system.

This was fine at first until the small sizes of the communities served allowed a few local dealers to monopolise and share out the fish sales between them, so as to control prices. Free auctions outside the larger central Brisbane market became controlled and profits fell. It is quite normal, however, for such markets to be operated as a community service and to lose money and to be subsidised by the taxpayer. Locally caught fish is needed but its value in a small town cannot support a market which is required for quality control purposes. Fish is a perishable commodity.

The east coast prawn fishery was in its early development phase and was highly profitable. The decision for the Fish Board to build and operate a prawn processing and export plant was taken in the belief that its profits would subsidise the fish auctions.

This kind of business in a highly competitive field cannot survive under a Government-owned regime, and should have been left to private enterprise. I recommended a sell-off of the venture, which was carried out many years later after a twelve million dollar loss was incurred, and long after I had left the scene.

In connection with the Fish Board it was reported in "The Courier-Mail" on 30th June 1987:

Government wants 12 million dollars for assets

The State Government is holding out for a better price for the Queensland Fish Board assets it has offered for sale.

Four companies, including one from interstate, have bid for the property which includes the markets in Brisbane.

The highest offer is understood to be about 6 million dollars. But the Treasury Department estimates the Board "owes" the public purse about 12 million dollars.

The Primary Industries Minister, Mr. Harper, said the Government was determined to obtain as close to the 12 million dollars as possible.

The matter which concerned me more at the time was the Spanish mackerel fishery. Mackerel were the most important fish resource on the Queensland coast and were caught by a large fleet of small vessels operating from all the harbours. The vessels were poorly equipped with inadequate refrigeration or ice boxes and the fish landed was often poor in quality. The fishing season was fairly short, calling for long storage periods ashore. Each port had its season and the boats did not follow the fish, fishing only locally.

In an attempt to remedy this situation, the Fish Board instituted a subsidy to help the small mackerel boats to install small freezers on board to allow them to stay at sea for longer and catch more fish. The freezers provided were inadequate in power to quick-freeze large fish such as mackerel, though large enough to store them, once frozen.

The predictable result of this policy was that a large glut of very poor quality fish filled the Fish Board's cold stores during the mackerel season, which often carried over into the following year.

Another result was to teach the public that mackerel was not a good buy, which was a disastrous policy for our best available bulk fish. The quality was ruined by the slow freezing and the long storage.

One enterprising Queensland fisherman, "Snowy" Whittaker, took advantage of this situation. He built a large vessel, the "Trader Horn" with powerful refrigeration, storage for tons of fish and able to carry five fishing dories and crews. He was able to stay at sea and follow the fish in their migrations until he had a full load. He was able to land almost half of the State's mackerel catch of good quality fish. This is the kind of operation that should have been subsidised instead of inadequate freezers on small boats. But I was told to keep my nose out of the Fish Board. The Fish Board did not like "Snowy" Whittaker. He delivered too much fish for them to handle at one time and caused a glut. Nevertheless, he was on the right track and was doing exactly what I had suggested the Fish Board should have encouraged.

FISH FARMING

Fishing activities close to the coast often occur in sight of the general public and cause complaints about killing too many juvenile fish or causing damage to the environment. Also a rising population and increased demand for fish puts more pressure on finite resources.

It was for reasons such as these that I used occasional speaking opportunities, and the media, to make comments about the future potential of fish farming. Trout and salmon farming were well established elsewhere and the farming of oysters and mussels were commonplace. The technical problems of prawn breeding to the juvenile stage were largely solved, but the cost of feeding them up to adult stages remained a problem, at least in Australia.

I wrote a paper for a Fishing Industry meeting in May 1972, in which I emphasised the rising world population and the increasing cost of food produced on the land. I predicted a rapid rise in the harvesting of marine products.

I continued with a brief description of the marine food chain, and pointed out that much of our harvest is taken from the highest trophic levels and from fish stocks already highly or over-exploited. Large increases in production would have to come from lower trophic levels which can support higher yields, from species not currently fished or from fish farming.

It is not generally understood that there is an energy loss of about an order of magnitude between each trophic level, or during the step from prey to predator. The food chain or food pyramid demonstrates this process in a mangrove area, for example, where bacteria and other microscopic creatures living on leaf litter and in the mud form the first level. These are the food source of the next trophic level comprising juveniles of many species followed by larger animals as the pyramid is climbed. This process requires about ten times the weight of food for each unit of product at each level.

The problems needing solutions were:

1. Processing of products to reduce distribution costs.
2. Advertising of new products.
3. Development and trial of new products.
4. Manufacture of cheap pelletised food to enable profitable fish farming to occur.
5. Exploration of deep water raft culture of molluscs, such as mussels.
6. Open water raft culture of fish to replace expensive pond culture.

Many of these ideas are now commonplace and profitable practices by which food production is keeping pace with population growth, but in 1972 they were just being investigated.

I was unable to get funding for research in this field, and I believed it was more a goal for private enterprise. I would have liked to pursue the idea of a fish farm raising two or more products to spread the costs of feeding during the juvenile to the adult or marketable stage, but when I was misquoted in "The Courier-Mail" in May 1972 as wanting to raise pearl oysters with prawns in Moreton Bay I gave up that approach.

The Sydney rock oyster grows well in Moreton Bay, whereas the pearl oyster grows in tropical water of the Torres Strait.

I managed to interest a large company in an experimental farm for tiger prawns and mud crabs in the Redland Bay area, but the time had not come. I was ahead of my time. Prawn, tuna and barramundi farming are now flourishing.

The primitive fish farms I was involved with in northern Ghana in the 1950s combined fish, pigs and irrigated small crops. These worked as extensions to water supply dams and weirs, which we were building in the dry parts of the country. They worked because of the low wage structure at local village level.

Two private naturalists in Queensland, Hamar Midgley and Gerald Cook, were engaged in breeding some species of sport fish to use in stocking water supply dams. I encouraged them in their efforts, but could not provide any direct assistance. I felt that this was work which the government should have been doing, but I had no funds to use for such purposes.

CHAPTER 13

BOATING & FISHERIES PATROL

Fisheries Inspectors are the eyes and ears of the Fisheries Administration. To do his job the Fisheries Manager must be in touch with the various groups of professional fishermen and anglers throughout the State, as well as keeping in touch with fish wholesalers, processors and exporters. Without this detailed information he is operating on experience instead of solid knowledge. Fisheries Inspectors stationed throughout the country, and patrolling constantly in their areas, maintain this flow of information through regular reports to Head Office.

In 1964 I had 11 inspectors, some of whom reached retiring age during the next two years, and I was able to get approval to replace these and add about four extra personnel to the team. None of these men had received any training in Fisheries matters, and a proper training scheme for such a small group was problematical at the time. They were enforcement officers collecting revenue for the Department.

In 1966 boating activities expanded rapidly throughout the State, particularly in the Moreton Bay region, and the use of fast speed boats by an untrained public was causing problems. The suggestion was made that the Water Police unit should be expanded to oversee private boating activities. On 16th February 1967, I submitted a counter proposal to establish a new Boating and Fisheries Patrol incorporating my existing inspectors. I developed this proposal to set up three regional areas, each under a Senior Inspector, with a Superintendent in charge in Brisbane. My scheme included a much-improved fleet of boats suited to their individual patrol areas, and a training scheme including regular training courses in Fisheries fieldwork, information gathering as well as enforcement.

This proposal was accepted enthusiastically by the Head of Department, and the Government. I was authorised to commence a programme of recruitment and to purchase equipment over a three year period, and the Boating and Fisheries Patrol came into existence.

In a previous chapter I mentioned that I was Chairman of the Education Committee (a sub-committee of the Standing Committee of Fisheries). I was able to incorporate my training scheme for Fisheries Inspectors into the regular scheme operated by the Education Committee. This achieved a firm basis for the training of the new field staff on an Australia wide basis.

Having achieved this innovation, and having overseen the establishment of the Boating and Fisheries Patrol, I felt I was moving forward at last against the bureaucratic opposition encountered in the past, but I was wrong.

Soon after the new Patrol was set up it became apparent that its Superintendent, Lou Stevenson, was reporting to the department head. I had lost control of the field officers, though I was still largely responsible for their training through the Education Committee.

About 1969 an announcement was made that Fisheries would be transferred to the Department of Primary Industries.

All the Fisheries files arrived in a wheelbarrow, and were dumped on the floor in the corridor outside the Fisheries office.

I made contact with the Head of the Department of Primary Industries, Dr. Jim Harvey, who said I should stay where I was for the time being until he could work things out. I found that the transfer instructions did not include the Boating and Fisheries Patrol, so I had now lost all my field staff. Quite possibly I was now the only Chief Inspector of Fisheries in the world without any Fisheries Inspectors. I now knew why my Head of Department, Harbours and Marine, had been enthusiastic about my Boating and Fisheries Patrol proposal. I believed that he knew that Fisheries was about to be transferred to DPI and that he would keep the vastly expanded Patrol which became a body mainly engaged in enforcement instead of Fisheries work.

This situation was not to last very long before an announcement appeared in the newspaper to the effect that Fisheries was to be transferred again to the Department of Harbours and Marine.

I protested to Dr. Harvey, who advised me to write a letter to the Chairman of the Public Service Board asking for an interview, which I did. In my letter and at the interview I made it clear that Fisheries was a scientifically based activity that should be housed in a scientifically based Department, and that the Department of Harbours and Marine was a revenue based Department, with no scientific involvement. Furthermore, I had made it clear that a fruitful working arrangement with the Head of that Department, an Accountant, with no knowledge of Fisheries, was no longer possible.

The Chairman of the Public Service Board told me that the transfer to the Department of Harbours and Marine would not proceed, and that Fisheries would be temporarily attached to the Office of the Minister for Conservation, Marine and Aboriginal Affairs, Neville Hewitt. For the next few months I worked directly with this Minister, without any departmental involvement. To do this it was necessary for him to give me certain delegations under the Fisheries Acts. This had certain interesting repercussions later.

After some time the Government confirmed that Fisheries would be permanently transferred to the Department of Primary Industries as an independent Branch responsible to the Director-General's office, and not working through one of the Divisions of the Department.

A new position was approved for me as Director of the Fisheries Branch during a departmental reorganisation in 1971, along with several other positions in other Branches. This was an incidental promotion rather than a personal one. Nobody appealed against my appointment.

The Fisheries Inspectors and the Boating and Fisheries Patrol were never restored to the Fisheries Branch. The ABC-TV "7:30 Report" on the 16th December 2009 described the Queensland Boating and Fisheries Patrol as having a 12 month training course and boats capable of travelling at 53 knots.

CHAPTER 14

CHARGE UNDER THE PUBLIC SERVICE ACTS

During my service with the Minister for Conservation, Marine and Aboriginal Affairs, Neville Hewitt, a highly controversial matter concerning dolphins was the subject of a media fuss. Keith Williams, the owner of Seaworld on the Gold Coast, had been developing his dolphin display, and was being attacked by conservationists claiming cruelty and making sundry other objections. I was involved in developing a minimum set of standards for dolphin pools which gave the animals an adequate amount of freedom. Keith Williams had recently constructed a new dolphin pool and needed about two more dolphins to complete his performance team. One day, after my transfer to the Department of Primary Industries, he rang me to say that suitable dolphins had been sighted near the South Passage Bar, and knowing that his facilities were up to standard I granted him a permit to collect two dolphins, acting on my delegated authority from the Minister for Conservation, Marine and Aboriginal Affairs.

A fresh outcry from the conservationists who opposed the Seaworld Dolphin Show resulted. The next morning I was called into the Director-General's Office by the Chief Administration Officer, (Lloyd Harris), in the absence of Dr. Jim Harvey, Director-General. In the office I was told to sit at the Board table where Alan Ross, the Acting Director-General was sitting, and then I was told by Alan Ross that I may be charged for exceeding my authority under the Fisheries Acts by granting licences to Keith Williams to take dolphins.

I produced my delegated authority which I always kept in my wallet with my authority card as Chief Inspector of Fisheries. Mr. Harris exclaimed "Oh he has got an authority"! This ended another attempt to get rid of me. I was not offered an apology, nor had I been told before the interview as to why I had been summoned to the meeting.

CHAPTER 15

TUNA SURVEY

During my travels in North Queensland and the Torres Straits I received many reports about tuna. Also there were repeated arrests of foreign tuna fishing vessels in northern Australian waters. I was able to collect some data on oceanographic currents and conditions in the area and, using my considerable experience in the tuna fishery off West Africa as a guide, I put together a report on the prospect of opening up a tuna fishery north of Cairns. I wrote a letter to the President of StarKist Sea Foods in California, one of the two largest tuna fishing companies in the USA at that time, seeking current information on costs of tuna processing and catching.

Mr. Joe Bogdanovic, later President of Heinz, and Mr. Nick Trutanic, Vice-President Operations of StarKist, arrived in Brisbane shortly afterwards. I had worked closely with them in the discovery and development of a large new tuna ground in the Gulf of Guinea off the West Coast of Africa. We discussed my ideas and they thought I was justified in predicting a new fishery in the northern Coral Sea.

There appeared to be a real opportunity to open up a tropical tuna fishery in North Queensland based on either bulk export of frozen tuna, or on a local cannery. A new market was opening for fresh large tuna, air-lifted overnight to Tokyo for the Sushi trade. This was interesting because of the very high prices of about $1000 per fish.

Geoff Harrison inspecting tuna.

Mr. Bogdanovich said he was not interested in an involvement by his Company at present, but he offered me a position as Manager of his Company's prawning operations in Kerala, India. I said that I was too committed to our family here in Queensland. When I left Ghana, StarKist had offered me a job to manage all of their bases in West Africa, but I declined because of the climate that I had already endured for 13 years.

I submitted my proposal to the Department and was asked to prepare a full commercial proposal, which I did. I then negotiated for a survey, using a tuna live bait boat chartered from the southern bluefin fleet and a spotter plane. The survey, controlled by the CSIRO, was financed by the Commonwealth Government and Queensland and lasted six months.

My request was for a survey in far northern waters outside the Great Barrier Reef between Cairns, Cape York and Samurai, particularly along the edge of the continental shelf during the summer months. This is the area in which many foreign tuna vessels had been arrested by Australian naval vessels for poaching in Australian waters.

The CSIRO insisted on searching the offshore reef areas between Rockhampton and Cairns in the winter months. I believe that their proposal was based on their knowledge of the southern bluefin tuna, a different species to the northern bluefin, yellowfin and skipjack which I expected to find. The survey was not successful and failed to find the tuna resources that I had predicted.

Many years later I read a newspaper report that the tuna fishery in Papua New Guinea had landed record tuna catches of about 250,000 tons from the northern areas. Large landings are also recorded by Australian boats.

I wondered at the time if the badly overfished southern blue fin tuna industry saw my survey as future competition, and I also wondered why my survey was carried out in the wrong place and at the wrong time of the year.

When Nick Trutanic, Vice-President Operations of Star Kist, invited me and my wife to dinner in Brisbane several years ago, he told us that his Company referred to the West African tuna grounds as "Harrison's Fishery".

CHAPTER 16

OCEANIC GRANDEUR

In March 1970 an oil tanker, fully laden with Sumatran crude oil, grounded on an un-charted reef adjacent to the Torres Strait Shipping Channel spilling some thousand tons of its cargo. The task of investigating this incident was taken out of my hands. My two Marine Biologists were sent to investigate.

I advised the Department at the time, however, that no dispersants should be used, and that the oil escaping the clean-up operation should be left to disperse naturally because:

1. The oil was floating and of light grade;
2. Tides and winds are strong in the area with rapid dispersal;
3. Sunlight evaporates the volatile components, which are the most harmful;
4. Coral exudes a protective slime which rejects oil; and
5. Little oil would penetrate the water mass where it may cause harm to living creatures.

My advice was ignored and it was ordered that a dispersant (Gamlen) be used. I was over-ruled again.

Gamlen is a surfactant which carries the oil down into the water mass and breaks it into small particles. These particles are carried along in the sea floor zone, until trapped by a filter feeding organism such as coral or molluscs. Each particle carries its harmful load indefinitely and is not subject to normal dilution laws. It also has an indeterminate range like a particle of silt.

Subsequent reports on damage to the pearl oysters were claimed to be unconnected with the oil spill. I believe that no firm data existed on which to base such claims. Certainly no research was conducted in this field. The claims and the decision to use Gamlen were based on opinions, not on research.

INDO PACIFIC FISHERIES COUNCIL

During my service in the Department of Primary Industries (1970-75), the Indo Pacific Fisheries Council, which included all the Pacific Nations as well as Australia, Japan, the UK and the USA, was scheduled to meet in Noumea. I was invited to be one of two main speakers by the Food and Agriculture Organisation of the United Nations in Rome, which was the convenor.

The Department of Primary Industries approved my participation and I prepared my talk on coral reef fisheries, organised my passport and had my inoculations. My air tickets were booked and a few days before departure I received a telephone call from the Chief Administration Officer of DPI, Lloyd Harris, telling me that I was not going. He would not give a reason.

I had to telephone the Food and Agriculture Organisation in Rome, and make my apologies, which left them without one of the two theme speakers at the Council meeting in Noumea.

Fortunately Colin Beaver, the Convenor and a man I knew well from my Ghana days, understood my problem.

CHAPTER 18

TORRES STRAITS SURVEY

In July 1973, the Queensland Cabinet approved a survey of the fish resources of the Torres Straits area. Two Biologists were appointed and two trawlers were chartered to carry out the work. At this time a treaty was being negotiated with Papua New Guinea to draw up the State boundaries, and there were numerous complaints arising from the alleged incursions of New Guinea fishermen into alleged Torres Straits Islanders traditional fishing grounds.

The survey was conducted by Mr. Rex Pyne, a highly experienced officer in the Papua-New-Guinea area, whom I recruited to conduct the survey which lasted about nine months, and covered prawns, crayfish and mackerel.

Mr. Pyne's report in three parts made an assessment of the three fisheries, which I passed on to the Government. The report, which made use of Rex Pyne's extensive previous work in the New

Guinea area, as well as the survey data, was comprehensive and valuable to Queensland and to Mr. Pyne's career path in research.

To my surprise Cabinet ordered that it be withheld and marked confidential. Rex Pyne, who wanted his work published, made his displeasure very clear and I felt that he blamed me for what had happened. Subsequently I found out that a member of my staff was at loggerheads with Mr. Pyne, and I wondered if this may have caused the problem.

It was not long after this that I was moved out of my position. Soon afterwards Rex Pyne resigned, which was a loss to the Department since he was a very good research officer.

CHAPTER 19

DEMOTION

The fishing industry is based on a hunting economy. The great diversity of activities related to fish and fishing, and the differences existing between hunting and farming economies and philosophies, demand that the Fisheries administration should be independent of other administrations.

Other States had Directors of Fisheries who reported directly to their Ministers, so it was time for Queensland to follow suit. Queensland also lacked an up-to-date Organisation to represent the Commercial Fishermen. The Professional Fishermen's League and the Trawlermen's Association did not fill this need. On several occasions the fishermen had spoken to me about it. They wanted a Body with full Industrial Union status which involved legislation under the State Industrial Laws. This involved me in more disagreements with the bureaucracy before the Queensland Commercial Fishermen's Organisation was formed.

In view of this, I had prepared and submitted, to the Government, a new structure for Fisheries Administration which was to be headed by a Minister for Fisheries at a sub-Department level. This would have more status than the existing Fisheries Branch and help satisfy the fishermen's demands, but had received no response or comment for a considerable period.

This proposal received strong support from the Queensland Commercial Fishermen's Organisation. The fishermen wanted a Minister with direct Fisheries responsibility, as much as I did, so as to get direct access to the Government on policy matters.

Out of the blue, about November 1974, I was instructed to take my long completed draft of the Fisheries Act to the Parliamentary Draftsman, when the Royal Commission into Oil Drilling on the Great Barrier Reef ended. Obviously the Government was happy to use my expertise before demoting me.

It will be recalled, in Chapter 4, Gulf of Carpentaria Prawn Survey, that Queensland passed amending legislation in November 1974, to clear the way for State licensing of processing plants.

It was also at this time that the Government announced its approval of my proposal to create a new Fisheries administrative structure, and to appoint the first Minister for Fisheries. The Hon. Claude Wharton, a farmer and grazier, was appointed in March 1975 as Minister for Aboriginal and Islanders Advancement, Fisheries and National Parks. He then became the first Minister for Fisheries in Queensland.

The Fisheries Branch was moved from the DPI and became the Queensland Fisheries Service on 27th May 1975.

I am of the opinion that my proposal to create a new Fisheries Administrative structure, with direct Ministerial access, was approved as a means of ousting me. By setting up a new Public Service Body, which they called the Queensland Fisheries Service, they were able to create non-appealable positions under the Public Service Acts.

It was reported in the "Nation Review" (24th April to 1st May 1975) that a renowned anti-conservationist was rumoured to become the No. 1 Fisheries Officer in Queensland. This was before any advertising for the position had taken place, but he was not accepted. The next person to be considered was from the Agricultural Bank, who was also rejected.

I met the Hon. Claude Wharton, farmer and grazier, through a chance meeting in George Street, who informed me on 27th May 1975, that I was no longer the Director of Fisheries. He told me the names of the new appointees and I told him that my replacements would not last much more than 12 months. They were replaced after 13 months.

Why was I sent a letter on **22nd May 1975,** appointing me Director, Fisheries Section, Queensland Fisheries Service, as from **27th March 1975?** Norm Hall and Ernest Grant were appointed (on the **27th May 1975)** to take charge of Fisheries. Was this gross incompetence or part of the war of denigration being waged against me? I never held this position.

Unfortunately, the first Director of Fisheries appointed under the new structure was an Economist (Agriculture), Norm Hall, who had no direct knowledge or experience in Fisheries. After 13 months, Norm Hall and his deputy, Ernest Grant, were replaced. Mr. Hall had been promoted about 11 classifications in approximately five years, to classification 19, and retained his rights when he became full time Chairman of the Fish Board in 1976.

A new position was created for Mr. Grant as Special Adviser (Marine Biology), Department of Harbours and Marine, and he retained his rights – he had been promoted to Classification 15.

The Minister responsible for Fisheries, the Hon. Mike Ahern, said, in his Foreword of this book that the ideal Fisheries Scientist (Manager) needs to be part-biologist, part economist, part-gear technologist, part-sociologist, part-lawyer. I would add he needs to be experienced in fish processing, marketing, and the needs of anglers and the general community. I claimed to be the best qualified in Queensland to Head the Queensland Fisheries Service. There was nobody in Queensland who could challenge me on technical grounds. In a story that I featured in on the ABC-TV "7:30 Report" broadcast on the 24th November 1988, Sir Thomas Hiley a former Queensland Treasurer and Minister said that he believed I was "scientifically miles ahead". That report is available for viewing at my website www.demonocracy.com.au.

At the end of 1992 I obtained a copy of Executive Minute B372A, through Freedom of Information, regarding the establishment and staffing arrangements for the Queensland Fisheries Service. The State Archives at Runcorn were unable to produce the Cabinet papers covering this matter under the 30 year rule, and after this period had expired.

I was demoted to a classification eight position, as Executive Officer, although I retained my salary classification of thirteen, but not my status. Furthermore, I was to be demoted in Executive Minute B372A BEFORE Cabinet approved the establishment of the Queensland Fisheries Service. In this Minute, Noel Melville Haysom was to become Assistant Executive Officer in 1975, junior to me.

These two positions of Executive Officer were not gazetted, although it was stated in Executive Minute B372A that notification of these appointments be published in the Government Gazette when they become effective.

In addition Executive Minute B372A stated that the position of Director, Queensland Fisheries Service also Chairman, Fish Board, be excluded from the Right of Appeal.

This did not include the position of Deputy Director of Fisheries, but in the Government Gazette of 16th April 1975, this position is non-appealable.

There were no discussions or explanations offered to me as to my demotion to number three most senior Fisheries Officer in Queensland from the number one position. Why was I kept in suspense for about five months as to my future from the time when the Royal Commission into Oil Drilling on the Great Barrier Reef ended in November 1974, and the announcement was made to appoint the first Minister for Fisheries (the Hon. Claude Wharton in March 1975)?

Why did I have to suffer the humiliation in 1975 of finding myself a seat at the end of the table in the Board Room, without a personal phone for Fisheries work, no staff, no budget and no set duties, in full view of my former staff, and with no explanation? Worse was to come.

As Executive Officer, I received a memorandum from the newly appointed Deputy Director of the Queensland Fisheries Service **(Ernest Grant)** dated 27th February 1976, **my former assistant, which instructed me –**

"Please refer attached correspondence regarding weekend closures in the Fitzroy River and estuary. Would you please prepare for the Director's signature on Monday, 1st March a form of Permit which will be sent to each of the nineteen fishermen listed in Mr. Reynolds' letter of 17th February, provided that each is licensed as a Master Fisherman. You will see that the area concerned relates to the Fitzroy River and estuary, and that the individual Permits will extend to 21st March "(Signed Ern Grant).

Norm Hall, (newly appointed Director of Fisheries) –

I rushed this through at about 4.30pm today (Friday) with the thought of giving Geoff a chance to assemble his thoughts and to do the background work of checking out fishing licences. Waste of time. Apparently Geoff looked in briefly in the a.m., and his "IN" tray has steadily built up all day. ? - did the GBRC (Great Barrier Reef Committee) meet today?

Yes they met that day, Mr. Hall! I had previously obtained approval to attend the meeting of the GBRC from the Director.

This memorandum was addressed to **me as newly appointed Executive Officer, Queensland Fisheries Service.** Not long before this I had told a Public Service Commissioner that I was virtually redundant.

Because I felt I was being deliberately provoked, I was forced to take long service leave although I was not financially prepared. I went to my relatives in England in March 1976, for about six months and took my family with me.

During this period I became aware that the positions of Director of Fisheries and Chairman of the Fish Board and, secondly, Deputy Director of Fisheries had become vacant. I wrote from England to the Public Service Board, but was informed that these positions were not advertised as being vacant.

I returned from England on a Saturday in September 1976, and on that night I received a phone call at home from Pat Killoran, Director, Department of Aboriginal and Islanders Advancement (DAIA), informing me that I would not be returning to the Queensland Fisheries Service. I was denied a reason. On the 14th September 1976, I was seconded to this Department and was informed that I was to be Fisheries Adviser. I found I had no set duties, no designation in DAIA, no staff, no specific Fisheries budget, and no telephone for several months. An office room was divided into three sections and I occupied a corner with office partition screens around me.

I set up projects in the Torres Straits, visited a crocodile farm at the Edward River and visited Palm Island regarding oyster farming. I also wrote several unsolicited reports.

A substantial report I prepared on the Torres Straits Fisheries was unused. I prepared a History of Queensland Fisheries covering the period from late last century until I took up duty on 28th February 1963, in Queensland. Again, this report was unsolicited.

It was not until 2nd June 1977, some nine months after my secondment to DAIA, that a position of Technical Advisory Officer (Fisheries) was created for me at Classification 13.

The Chairman of the Public Service Board stated on 20th May 1977 –

"Upon this position being vacated by Mr. Harrison, the question of a reassessment of classification and designation should be submitted to this Department before any action is taken to fill the position.

The position of Clerk Administration (Stores), Kowanyama, should be deleted from the establishment of the Department of Aboriginal and Islanders Advancement)."

When I was Director of Fisheries Pat Killoran, Director of DAIA, was a colleague of mine. He was mentioned in the Queen's Honours List in 1977 and had much pleasure in showing me his medal.

Through Freedom of Information, I discovered that when I was on leave in England in 1976, Mr. Killoran had applied for a transfer from Fisheries, on my behalf, without my knowledge, which was approved. He then implemented this as a secondment. An enforced transfer can be construed as a punishment. I believe that I was treated as an accused.

On 30th September 1976, I sought an interview with the Minister Hon. Claude Wharton, in order to clear my name and to restore my professional reputation, at a national and an international level, earned through 26 years in this field.

The Minister said he knew of nothing against me, and that my assessment of the two officers who replaced me in 1975 was correct. The Minister added that the original appointments were decided before he was appointed as Minister of the Crown, and after his appointment he became aware of the situation and was unable to do anything about it.

Minister Wharton said he was aware that senior officers in the public service were antagonistic towards me. He asked me what I would achieve if I was able to refute the allegations that had been made against me, and I said re-appointment as Director of Fisheries. The Minister said that the Public Service officers concerned would still be antagonistic towards me, and they would interfere in many ways with the smooth running of the Fisheries organisation.

I said that as Director of the QFS I would be working directly with him as Minister and not, as in the past, working through a senior officer who was antagonistic towards me. The Minister said that this did not prevent senior officers of other government departments from holding things up, and cited the new Fisheries Bill as a particular case.

I asked for an opportunity to face my accusers but this was denied me. I said I had achieved a lot over the years against the opposition of these people, and could continue to do so. There was no way they could oppose me on technical grounds. The Minister added that, whilst I was free to apply for appointment when the positions of Director and Deputy Director of the Queensland Fisheries Service were advertised in the future, he felt that the Cabinet decision was such as to preclude me from consideration for the various reasons stated above.

When I was appointed to take up duty in Queensland in 1963, and when I was promoted in 1971 in the DPI to Classification 13, as the result of staff adjustments involving seven people, I was required to have the necessary scientific qualifications and experience. Since 1975 when Fisheries was "upgraded", senior appointments have been made regardless of qualifications and experience.

Mr. Noel Haysom, a former member of my staff, wrote in "Trawlers, Trollers and Trepangers", which he authored, and which was published by the DPI in 2001:

> "Eventually, however, Killoran realised that he had to take some action to lighten Hall's load, and to get someone whom he knew and trusted into the top position of the QFS".

(My picture appears on the previous page of his book and obviously Mr. Haysom considered that Mr. Killoran didn't trust me, or so it seems to me).

His decision, made nearly a year after the creation of the service, was announced with little warning and came as a sudden shock to many people, including myself. I received a phone call from Killoran's office one midmorning, summoning me to his presence immediately.

Not knowing the reason for the summons, I was, during my city-block walk to his office, going over in my mind various possible sins of commission or omission without arriving at any really sensible explanation of this reason for the sudden call.

On entering Killoran's office, I found the Minister's Private Secretary, Cornelius (Con) Reardon, already present, which only worried me to think that some crisis of political significance had suddenly occured, and I probably had not yet even heard of it! Killoran asked me to sit down, and then wasted no time in saying in general terms, 'We are making a few changes in Fisheries. Mr. Hall is going to take over the full-time control of the Fish Board. Mr. Reardon will be the new director of QFS, and you will act as his deputy. I expect you to act as his technical adviser, but I also want you to give priority to getting the proposed new Fisheries Act ready for presentation to Parliament.

Reardon knew nothing about fisheriers, apart from what he may have learned indirectly during the previous year in his role as the Minister's Private Secretary. But he had been Killoran's trusted deputy for many years ..."

I, Geoff Harrison, always believed that the Public Service Acts required that the appointee should be the best-qualified applicant, that is, appointments should be made on merit.

By 1977, my two former Assistants, Ernest Grant and Noel Haysom, had become senior to me in the Public Service.

Regarding Con Reardon's appointment it was reported in "The Professional Officer" (The Union Journal), March/April 1977, as follows:

"The salary difference is 8,800 dollars per annum. Academic qualifications of appointment (None were shown). Appointments such as this leave questions to be answered –

(a) The appointee will head a Technical Division comprised essentially of Technical Officers – yet he does not hold Technical qualifications himself. This was unusual to say the least. Surely Technical Officers on higher qualifications and with in-depth Technical expertise and administrative ability were available to fill this position. Persons both inside and outside the Service must view such an appointment at face value as being not only incredible but very questionable.

(b) Why was a person on a 1 (6) classification appointed as Acting as a 1 (17) classification? Was it to allow that person to be given experience and to be fitted into the 1 (17) position? This is apparently what happened. How fair is this to other officers?

(c) What criteria were used for selection of the appointee? Of course the Government might argue that with no right of appeal perhaps no justification is required."

The Professional Officers' Association responded that regarding the Appointment to Director, Queensland Fisheries Service, as members will be aware in the March/April issue of the Association Journal, the Association questioned the appointment of the above position. A number of members in the Queensland Fisheries Service, mainly through their Councillor, have expressed the following opinion:

1. The appointee has held senior positions previously and has a high degree of administrative experience.
2. Previous Directors did not hold specific Fisheries Biology qualifications, and
3. The person appointed has proved to be effective in the position and is generally well liked by staff.

The Association has raised the issue as one of principle – we do not question the capabilities of the appointee. What concerns the Association is the appointment of non-technically qualified officers to senior positions in technical areas and the use of acting appointments to allow officers to gain experience culminating in their subsequent permanent appointment to the position. It is for these reasons that we published the open letter to the Minister. In hindsight the Association realises that it would have been advantageous to have had discussions with the Councillor prior to publishing the article and this oversight is regretted. However, the Association sees this matter as one of Principle and not Personalities.

On 25th August 1981, I received a letter from the Honourable Mike Ahern, an extract of which reads:

"I was never able to understand the events of the history of your involvement in fisheries policy. I am very sorry that now it is my responsibility, you are not involved. I always had a very high regard for your ability."

The State Secretary of the Queensland Commercial Fishermen's State Council wrote on 26th March 1975, inter alia:

"We wish to acknowledge, with thanks, the co-operation of your Director of Fisheries, Mr. G. G. T. Harrison, and we look forward to further discussions with him on what the Queensland Commercial Fishermen's State Council would like to have included in the 1975 Fisheries Act."

In 1975, Mr. Nutter, General Secretary of the Professional Officers' Association, telephoned me expressing his concern about the changes to the position of Director of Fisheries, and indicated to me that, if the new position of Director of Fisheries and Chairman of the Fish Board had not been non-appealable, he would have employed a Barrister to defend my position.

When I was on leave in England I received a letter dated 4th August 1976, from the General Secretary of the Professional Officers' Association, which read:

"I acknowledge receipt of your letter of 16th July 1976, concerning the Queensland Fisheries Service, and wish to advise that I am currently investigating the total situation in respect to this matter. If I were to say that I am surprised at the Acting appointment I would be understating my concern. I will let you know if anything eventuates." ("The Professional Officer" March/April 1977 refers).

Why did the Professional Officers' Association change its attitude from one of support for me by May-June 1977, in the space of two months?

Regarding the appointment of Director of Fisheries and Chairman of the Fish Board in 1975, Mr. Nutter's assistant, Professional Officers' Association, advised me to take no action until the appointment was confirmed, and then, if necessary, I could approach the Ombudsman. This gentleman would have known that the Ombudsman couldn't question a Cabinet decision. When I approached the Ombudsman I was unsuccessful. I made the approach even though I believed he couldn't question a Cabinet decision.

Con Reardon, appointed Acting Director of Fisheries in 1976, was a good administrator and a gentleman, and it was known he was not well and was expected to retire within a short time. At the time the rumour was that he would retire after two years with increased superannuation.

When I was appointed in February 1963, to take charge of Queensland Fisheries as the first occupant of a new job, one of the reasons I was brought here from "Outside" was because there were no trained, experienced Fisheries Managers in Queensland.

The late Sir Thomas Hiley, former Treasurer and Minister responsible for Fisheries stated on the ABC-TV "7:30 Report" broadcast on the 16th December 1988:

"He (Harrison) was not with me long enough to form any great impression, but he was 'scientifically miles ahead'. I had no complaint with him, but I was forced to show some interest when I discovered that there was a bitter war of denigration being waged against him."

John Austin, the reporter said:

"As for Mr. Harrison's claim that he was shut out of advising the Premier, Sir Thomas recounts how the chumminess of the Public Service could operate, and how a former Fisheries Adviser - not Harrison – made his representations at Premier level."

Sir Thomas Hiley continued:

"Normally, he would not have had great access, but these things can be advanced. I know he was quite friendly with the Under-Secretary of the Department, Keith Spann, a man whom I knew well and saw a lot of – he used to take Spann fishing and supply him with fish – and various other ways which I rather sensed may be a bit of ingratiation."

That report is available for viewing at my website www.demonocracy.com.au.

Section 38 of the Public Service Regulations of 1958 state, inter alia, "Outside Influence. Officers are prohibited from seeking the influence or interest of any person in order to obtain promotion, transfer, or other advantage…".

Keith Spann signed the Executive Minute whereby I lost my career, and in which I was reduced to number three Fisheries Officer in Queensland, from number one, BEFORE Cabinet approved the establishment of the Queensland Fisheries Service.

Keith Spann was mentioned in the Honours List of 1980 for outstanding and distinguished service as an officer of the Crown.

When Con Reardon retired, Noel Melville Haysom, my former Assistant, stepped into his shoes in 1978, and became Director of Fisheries in 1978, Classification 17, again senior to me.

In "Trawlers, Trollers and Trepangers", which Noel Haysom authored, and which the Department of Primary Industries published in 2001, under the heading of "The author's own tenure as Director, QFS", Mr. Haysom wrote:

> "I generally enjoyed my tour of duty as head of the State's fisheries governing body, although there were times when I felt that I was making drastic mistakes and some situations when I had no confident idea as to what I should be doing!
>
> I had the good fortune to have as deputy director, an experienced administrative warhorse from the DPI, Avery 'Joe' Winterton. He had been a candidate for the position of director, but probably missed out because his previous experience lay in fields other than fisheries."

Avery 'Joe' Winterton told me that he did not intend to apply for the position, but did so only because he knew that I (Harrison) would not be getting the number one Fisheries position.

Having been appointed as Director of Fisheries, QFS, in 1978, Mr. Haysom quoted in his book that the scene changed a little in the early 1980s, when Fisheries was transferred once again to DPI, and by that time the Director-General of the Department was Dr. Graham Alexander. Mr. Haysom went on to say:

> "At about this time, Dr. Alexander, in his endeavours to reform his Department to cope with changing situations in the Primary Industries world, was faced with the situation that one of his major departmental responsibilities (that of dairying) was rapidly declining in importance, while that of Fisheries was obviously about to boom. To maintain a reasonable balance within the departmental structure, quite understandably, he

decided to amalgamate Dairying and Fisheries into a single division within the Department, under the control of the then Director of the Division of Dairying, David Mitchell. Dave Mitchell knew virtually nothing about Fisheries, but he was an experienced public service manager, knew his way around the internal politics of the QDPI, and was familiar with Dr. Alexander's style of management. He and I had known each other for a long time, dating back to a sporting relationship on the hockey field in our undergraduate days, and together I think we formed a good team to oversee the transition period from the demise of the Queensland Fisheries Service as an independent body, and the development of an entirely new management infrastructure".

There is no connection between Fisheries and Dairying or cows, milk quotas and artificial insemination, or hens and hen quotas.

In regard to the upgrading of Fisheries in 1975, with the appointment of the first Minister for Fisheries, it will be seen that the status of Fisheries in 1981, with many appointments and promotions (except for me), at great cost to the taxpayer, was the same –

From 1971–75

Fisheries was known as   -   Fisheries **Branch**

From 1975

Fisheries was known as   -   Queensland Fisheries Service

From 1981

Fisheries was known as   -   Fisheries Service **Branch**

Up to 1975

There was a Specialist Adviser with no access to a Minister for Fisheries for him to advise

From 1975–77

There was a Minister for Fisheries with no specialist adviser (the Hon. Vic Sullivan, DPI, was the Minister responsible for Fisheries until March 1975)

From 1978 there was no Minister for Fisheries

It is a well-known fact that Fisheries Managers should grow up in Fisheries, not just step in to take charge. I understand that a Minister should be advised by a Specialist Adviser according to the Statute of Westminster.

After almost 20 years' service in Queensland, I made the decision it was time for me to go home to Manly for good and left on 6th August 1982, but not before taking home my morning tea mug, "Help I'm Trapped In The Establishment" - a present from my wife, Eunice, in 1976. The Senior Administration Officer wrote to the Director of DAIA on 7th July 1982 stating that Mr. Harrison has advised of his retirement as on 6th August 1982 and that his services have been continuous since 28th February 1963, and without disciplinary action.

My going away present was a very large card signed by many members of the staffs of Fisheries and the Department of Aboriginal and Islanders Advancement, which I value, together with a telegram.

The contrasts with our farewell African party when my wife and I, and my deputy Gordon Rawson, retired from Ghana were most marked. Our staff turned on a big show and the Chief of the Ga State as well as the Chief Fisherman and the head of the market women attended.

Mr. Jim Varghese, Queensland Director-General of the Department of Primary Industries and Fisheries, wrote to me on 21st July 2005, inter alia, stating "The department acknowledges your valuable contribution during the pioneering days of the Queensland fishing industry and in particular your contribution to sustainable use of fisheries resources and the critical fisheries habitat on which they depend."

It will be seen that the promotions that took place after 1975, along with transfers, creation of new posts, increased staff, and associated superannuation payments, would have cost the taxpayer an incalculable amount, particularly bearing in mind that the positions of Director of Fisheries were filled in 1975, 1976, 1977, 1978 and 1981.

Between 1975 and 1982 there were many promotions and I was the only senior Fisheries Officer who didn't receive a promotion. Why wasn't I reinstated when my successor was replaced in 1976? After all I was the one who had set it all up during the previous twelve years and three months as the first occupant of a new position.

Were any of the appointees in 1975, and since, trained and experienced in the Commercial Fisheries field? If so, who?

I understand that about 1983 the Queensland Fisheries Management Authority was set up with Inspectors, followed by the Fish Promotion Advisory Committee – a sub-committee with its own secretariat and separate board status, whose main function, it has been stated, seemed to be to make recommendations to the Queensland Fisheries Management Authority.

This was followed by the creation of a position of Director, Fisheries Management, Department of Primary Industries, along with other positions in DPI.

Rumours abounded in regard to the setting up of the Queensland Fisheries Management Authority – Dave Mitchell was in charge. He was supposed to be responsible to the Minister for Primary Industries. One of the purposes in setting it up, if it worked with the Minister, was to cut red tape, and get things done more quickly. In fact it still worked through the Department Head and his office.

Dave Mitchell and about half of his staff were public servants on secondment, and about the other half transferred, no longer public servants, employed only by the Authority.

According to the rumours, the purpose of setting up the Queensland Fisheries Management Authority was so that when all the trouble in the fishing industry subsided they could wind up the Queensland Fisheries Management Authority and transfer its functions back to the Department in an expanded management authority.

Furthermore, the Authority was created so as to set up somebody else to take brickbats from the fishermen, and had nothing to do with the future of the fishing industry. It was a means of protecting the Government from strife. Fishermen had a seat on the Authority and they thought the Authority was doing everything for them, letting them into closed areas, which would upset the tourist body – the number of trawlers in the Gulf would be reduced by restricting new licences and introducing a buy-back scheme until the fishermen received compensation for the loss of licences.

The rumour continued that the Authority gets the blame for clamping down on things like crayfishing in the Torres Strait or opening areas that were closed to fishing up and down the coast. The Government does not get the blame when the Authority has been used as a shield.

A leading South-East Queensland fisherman, Bob Greenhill, was quoted in the "Sunday Sun" on 18th March 1990:

"Industry problems such as pollution and market promotions are given only superficial attention – behind the scenes nothing seems to be going on."

He said the Government should scrap the QFMA (Queensland Fisheries Management Authority), and review the QCFO (Queensland Commercial Fishermen's Organisation).

Mr. Greenhill said most QFMA operations duplicated those of the Department of Primary Industry.

Mr. Greenhill said the QCFO had become bitterly divided and more than 2000 fishermen in the south-east corner were disturbed over its operations and those of the QFMA.

Both were operating like quangos – more interested in survival than in positively promoting the industry, he said.

In "The Courier-Mail" of 17th/18th May 2008, Des Houghton, Assistant Editor wrote:

Gradually and without warning, Australia's politicians have surrendered power to a bunch of unelected nobodies.

These nobodies run committees, commissions and authorities, administering billions in public funds. And their actions are rarely scrutinised.

Retired High Court judge, Ian Callinan, QC, commented on the power shift recently in Quadrant magazine.

He said some corporatised bodies seemed to have "a complete legal separation from the executive (government)".

"Under the Westminster system, ministers must be members of Parliament," he said. "The heads of statutory and corporatised bodies are however, not parliamentarians, and many have become, in Realpolitik, independent of ministerial control."

By the use of such authorities, (government) manages to deflect questioning and criticism to which it might otherwise be subjected," he said. "This is common. The chairs of many of these bodies court the media; almost all employ media officers. Frequently they exhort, cajole and admonish members of the public and those over whom they exercise power.

"They become, in short, political players, without political accountability."

Callinan blamed this "devolution of power", in part, on the corporatisation of government departments.

These unelected groups wield enormous power and their decisions have a profound impact on our lives.

In other words, gutless politicians have handed over our democracy to faceless bureaucrats.

So, who was responsible for blocking the Queensland Fishing Industry, and me?

Who, in a position of power, supported and promoted this person?

On the 19th December 1988, I received a letter from Sir Thomas Hiley, former Treasurer and former Minister responsible for Fisheries written from his home in Tewantin, which read in part –

"My Dear Geoffrey, In the A.B.C. interview I had good cause to lose regard for … (name supplied). He was bad in behaviour and his attempt to challenge your appointment was scandalous."

CHAPTER 20

TRAWLERS, TROLLERS and TREPANGERS

"Trawlers, Trollers and Trepangers", authored by Noel Haysom, a former member of my staff, and published in 2001 by the Department of Primary Industries in Queensland - General Disclaimer – "The Department of Primary Industries, Queensland has taken all reasonable steps to ensure that the information contained in this publication is accurate at the time of production".

Although I have lived at my current address for the past 54 years, DPI never approached me about this book. I was never given any drafts to peruse, my advice was not sought.

Needless to say it does not reflect the true record of my service in Queensland from 1963 until 1982, including Officer-in-Charge of Queensland Fisheries for 12 years and three months.

In "Trawlers, Trollers and Trepangers" Mr. Haysom refers to Fisheries Managers. Both he and Ernest Grant were Marine Biologists when I was appointed in 1963. They were not trained Fisheries Managers with commercial fisheries experience, they were working primarily as taxonomists.

That book seemed to me to be an attempt to wipe my "career" out of the record. The first big commercial fisheries project, the Gulf of Carpentaria Prawn Survey, commenced in Queensland soon after I took up duty in 1963, yet Mr. Haysom's book omits to mention my work in this regard.

Similarly, he omits to mention my work in connection with the Crown of Thorns Starfish, although I told the Committee of Inquiry, 1970, that **I considered the cause of the plague to be man-made, pollution. A view now generally accepted.**

In connection with the first system of Catch-and-Effort Statistics, Log Books, Mr. Haysom wrote on page 97 of his book, "I had become increasingly involved in monitoring the growing prawn fishery, in which I established Queensland's first system of catch-and-effort statistics".

As Head of Fisheries, I (Harrison) obtained approval to establish the first catch-and-effort statistics in the prawning industry in Queensland through a system of log books. This involved me in much negotiation with my Department and the Commonwealth Fisheries authorities, since most of the fishing took place outside Queensland waters. I then delegated Mr. Haysom to carry out this work.

"Other Queensland Fisheries Boffins" – on page 104 Mr. Haysom stated

> "Over the next few pages, I will comment on QFS officers whose selection for special mention by me has been heavily influenced by their years of service, compatibility with me, and a whole series of other factors."

I, Geoff Harrison, do not appear in this list so obviously Mr. Haysom does not agree with the comments of the late Sir Thomas Hiley on the ABC-TV "7:30 Report" broadcast on the 16th December 1988 who said that I was **"scientifically miles ahead"**. The full story can be viewed on my website, www.demonocracy.com.au

"Rape of Noosa (Canal development)" – I am the only Queensland Government officer mentioned by name by Mr. Haysom and indexed in his book under pages 81 and 82 "The Rape of Noosa". On page 82 he said:

"It seems somewhat extraordinary that anyone would suggest that fisheries managers would trade off an important stance in favour of some very minor administrative advantage." (The use of the Munna Point building).

Nancy Cato said in her book, "The Noosa Story":

"Was it merely coincidence that in 1974, soon after Noosa Sound was opened by the Premier, the Government built a new, white-brick headquarters for the fisheries inspectors, in a prime position on the river bank at Munna Point?"

On page 82 of "Trawlers Trollers and Trepangers", Mr. Haysom stated that although I was the bearer of the title of Chief Inspector of Fisheries I had no control over the Boating and Fisheries Patrol. In fact, since 1971 my designation was Director of Fisheries.

I, Geoff Harrison, had nothing to do with the establishment of a brand-new, white brick headquarters for the fisheries inspectors, who remained with the Boating and Fisheries Patrol in the Department of Harbours and Marine. I never set foot on this

Munna Point land and I was never in the building. I understand there was an accommodation flat in this building and a sea going boat that would not have been required on the Noosa River.

I was indexed in Mr. Haysom's book a second time for the "Rape of Noosa (Canal development)"; as well as on page 160, it is stated on page 150 "For his (Geoff Harrison) involvement in the environmental, scientific and administrative scenes see Chapter 9, 11 and 12." Chapter 9 is the Rape of Noosa.

On page 80, Chapter 9, "Trawlers Trollers and Trepangers", Mr. Haysom went on to say "But let us get back to a discussion of the environment and its role in fisheries management." Mr. Haysom added that he didn't intend to review the situation state wide, but merely comment on one of the local problem areas that were a classic environmental disaster (The Noosa River System).

Mr. Haysom omitted to say in "Trawlers, Trollers and Trepangers", as follows, which was an extract from Nancy Cato's book, "The Noosa Story" page 124:

> "One whole section of the findings of the coastal management investigators (Mr. Peter Waterman and Ms Stella Sabljak) dealing with 'case studies of recreational land use and availability of public space at Noosa and Caloundra' seems to have been suppressed; or, as an official of the Coordinator General's Department put it, "We didn't act upon it." It was not issued along with the other findings to the Steering Committee appointed by the councils involved.

> I have it on good authority that the copies circulated to the various heads of departments in the Lands Administration were all called in and destroyed. One, however, remained in the

Coordinator General's library, and I have obtained a copy of this. Even before the findings were issued, according to one of the investigators, 'heavy pressure' was put upon them not to offend big business in the form of land developers, especially of canal estates. The pressure came from the top downwards – from the Treasurer's Department of the Queensland Government."

As stated in a previous chapter on Mangroves (Chapter 9), I believe I was the first person in Australia to show the importance of the preservation of mangroves to provide food and shelter for fish, and to filter polluted water run-off from the land. I presented a paper to the Australian Conservation Foundation, at Queensland University, in October 1967, "Caring for Queensland". Mr. Haysom omitted this paper from the bibliography in his book.

I believe that Mr. Haysom's book has been widely circulated in Public Libraries and in Historical Societies, and that it was also circulated on the internet. I tried on many occasions to find out from DPI and Fisheries the full extent of the circulation of "Trawlers, Trollers and Trepangers". I was unsuccessful.

It was reported in "The Sun", 16th June **1989**, Brisbane GP Dr. Charles Russell, was awarded the Order of Australia for services to angling. The article stated that his role in fish management and conservation has been rewarded.

Dr. Russell went on to say:

"We're also involved in the preservation of the State's wetlands, and brought about the gradual education of the public and governments on the value of fish habitats."

I introduced the first fish habitat reserves in Queensland in Moreton Bay in January **1969, not** Dr. Russell.

Mr. Haysom stated in "Trawlers, Trollers and Trepangers"

"A move in the right direction was made following the 1957 Act with the introduction of fish habitat reserves…"

These were NOT Habitat reserves, they were fish nurseries in which all fishing was banned but not other activities or the destruction of mangrove trees. These were protected to the extent that a permit was needed to harvest mangrove poles for oyster farming.

On page 134 of his book, Section 18, Mr. Haysom stated:

"The Fisheries Act 1976, with its amending Acts (dated 1981 and 1982) introduced widespread changes into the Queensland fisheries management regime."

On page 135 Mr. Haysom added:

"Extension of reserve and sanctuary concepts to encompass Fisheries Habitat Reserves and Marine Parks…".

I drafted this Fisheries Bill between 1968 and 1974. Noel Haysom was told by the Director of DAIA, Pat Killoran in 1976, to give priority to getting the proposed new Fisheries Act ready for presentation to Parliament.

Furthermore, from "Trawlers, Trollers and Trepangers", in regards to the crown-of-thorns starfish plague, Mr. Haysom wrote:

"We sought assistance from the University of Queensland, and obtained their agreement that the project would be supervised by Dr. Robert Endean, who was an expert in marine toxicology, and of course was quite familiar with the crown-of-thorns starfish, which is a notorious marine stinger.

As a toxicologist it could hardly be claimed that he was really an expert in coral reef ecology. But I believe the biggest problem he had indischarging his responsibilities as the supervisor of the initial investigation was that (not being a practised public servant) he had no experience in how to phrase a report which was directed, not to his scientific peers, but to Government Ministers on a matter which would possibly have been gobbledegook to most of them, and which involved a recommendation for the expenditure of hundreds of thousands of dollars to resolve!"

Dr. Endean was a world-renowned expert on toxic marine animals, particularly in the coral reef area, and had a lifetime of research and diving on the Great Barrier Reef. His knowledge of coral and coral sea animals was comprehensive. Dr. Endean's book, "Australia's Great Barrier Reef" in 1982, was a valuable contribution to coral reef knowledge, obviously written by an expert.

In 2015 Dr. Endean was posthumously honoured with the naming of the Bob Endean Reef off the Far North Queensland coast, east of Mission Beach in recognition of his pioneering research into crown-of-thorns starfish infestation and the ecology and toxicology of marine organisms.

The UQ News published on February 4th 2015:

"UQ Institute of Molecular Biosciences', Professor Richard Lewis, who completed his PhD in marine toxins under Dr. Endean's supervision, said Dr. Endean was an outspoken advocate for the protection of the Great Barrier Reef.

"Bob had a visionary approach to science that often took him into heated debate with his peers," Professor Lewis said.

"One example was his research into crown-of-thorns starfish infestations, which he claimed were exacerbated by human impacts.

"The early criticisms from his detractors eventually turned full circle when the scale of the problem became more widely recognised."

Dr. Endean obtained a PhD from UQ in 1958 and worked in the University's Zoology Department for 40 years until his retirement in 1990.

He died in October 1997, aged 71, while on Heron Island – the launching pad for much of his research – where he was to deliver a keynote address to the 75th anniversary meeting of the Australian Coral Reef Society."

CHAPTER 21

ACCOUNTABILITY – WHISTLEBLOWERS

Dr. William de Maria said in the "Sunday Mail" on 10th September 1995 in regard to the whistleblower:

"So if they can't kill the persons off by making them have a breakdown or through a punitive transfer, they refuse them promotion or just relocate them to do something like counting staples into boxes all day."

Dr. de Maria was then a lecturer at Queensland University in social work and an expert in the field.

Des Houghton, Assistant Editor of "The Courier-Mail" wrote in the 24-25th March 2007 edition:

Transparency or Just an Illusion?

Claims of transparency and accountability by the State Government are a sham, according to a veteran public servant who worked in the state integrity unit.

Former State public servant Mark Lauchs says transparent and accountable government is just an illusion with little backing from the political bigwigs.

Mr. Lauchs says most accountability institutions set up by governments are designed to "give the illusion of Government transparency while operating to mask bad management or corruption".

Lauchs, 42, says most of the laws are "for show".

"There was no serious intent to make these things work," he says.

"The whistleblower legislation is more for show than to encourage disclosures.

"The Government has been hypocritical in Parliament; it never really supported whistleblower protection."

He says Police Minister Judy Spence and former health minister Wendy Edmond were outwardly hostile to whistleblowers in comments they made in Parliament.

Lauchs is now an Associate Professor with the Queensland University of Technology Faculty of Law, School of Justice. He spent three years studying accountability in the public service. Des Houghton's article continues:

After working in the Justice Department and the Premier's Department under four Premiers, Lauchs concludes:

"A Government does not have to be accountable as long as they can convince the voters they are honest."

He says Sir Joh Bjelke-Petersen worked with an Auditor-General and set up the Ombudsman system and the Financial Administration and Audit Act of 1977.

"These made sure the books balanced across Queensland, but did not and could not have exposed the endemic corruption which was kept under the radar," he says.

Lauchs said the same tactics were used after the Fitzgerald Inquiry.

The Government can claim credit for having a Freedom of Information Act but its effectiveness has been diluted through exemptions for Cabinet or Executive Council "considerations".

"This means Government can effectively put a sensitive document out of harm's way and make it inaccessible to the public for 30 years," Lauchs says.

He adds it is possible to disguise corruption using FOI exemptions. Deals of major financial payments are kept from public eyes under commercial-in-confidence rules.

"Another example is the Public Sector Ethics Act of 1994. Sounds good, but it carries ethical obligations without sanctions, and does not set benchmarks for success. The Act does not actually increase the likelihood of misconduct being revealed or prevented," says Lauchs. He believes Premier Peter Beattie has neglected a key whistleblower obligation.

"Under the Whistleblower Protection Act the Premier must report every year on the administration of the Act in his annual report," he says.

"It's never been done".

"I pointed this out and got a nasty reply from the Premier saying, basically, piss off."

Lauchs published his research as part of his PhD on the history of public sector ethics and accountability in Queensland. He described it to Des Houghton for the above article as "a PhD in the bleeding obvious".

From "The Bulletin" magazine published on the 18th November 1980:

OMBUDSMAN - The Bureaucracy...Who Guards the Guardians?

"In transplanting a Scandinavian idea and imposing it on our Westminster system, Australian Governments left out a provision which ensures people know ombudsmen are doing their jobs. In Scandinavia, but not in Australia, complainants and the Press have access to ombudsmen's files."

It was stated, inter alia, in the Editorial of "The Courier-Mail" of 29th March 2007:

Another Nail in the Name of Secrecy

"The Beattie Government is particularly prone to exercising control over the information flow, beginning with its excessive abuses of Freedom of Information laws by earmarking trolley-loads of material for Cabinet to gain secrecy status. Its large parliamentary numbers have given it breathtaking arrogance in pursuing cover-up and abandoning accountability: to the extent that it tried to censor the health inquiry when it learned that Commissioner Geoff Davies was planning to criticise the Government for its "culture of concealment" which hid hospital waiting lists.

With breathtaking arrogance, the Beattie Government claims it is best placed to decide what is and what is not in the public interest.

It changed legislation to give parliamentarians freedom to lie.

Now the Government has used its numbers to erode whistleblower protection laws by adding to parliamentary rules "guidelines" which warn MPs to avoid saying anything about a whistleblower case which could interfere with an investigation or cause unnecessary damage to a reputation."

CHAPTER 22

QUESTIONS THAT NEED TO BE ANSWERED

It was reported in the "Australian" on the 8th April 1971, as follows:

Old Laws Strangle Fishing Industry

"The perennial legal, administrative and practical problems besetting Queensland's 10 million dollar to 15 million dollar fishing industry seem no nearer to solution this year than they were last year.

At the same time the industry is booming, mainly because of prawning in the Gulf of Carpentaria off Weipa and Karumba. Industry estimates expect the Gulf to gross seven million dollars worth of prawns this year.

The industry's development is bottle-necked by archaic laws, no recognisable policy, and dissension within the industry. The weakness of the industry because of these factors makes it unrivalled in Australia..............and one of the weakest Fisheries Departments and Fishing Acts in any part of Australia."

It was reported in the "Sunday Sun", inter alia, on the 26th February 1989:

Fish Research Lags Badly

"Queensland is about 30 years behind the rest of Australia and overseas countries in fisheries research, according to a Canadian expert..." "It was a real shock to me when I came here and learnt so little had been done in Queensland" Professor Walters said. Professor Walters, from the University of British Columbia, was one of the speakers at a scientific workshop to discuss the effects of fishing in the Great Barrier Reef region.

Why did I have to accept the blame for the period covering my years of service from 1963-75?

When I arrived in Queensland in February 1963, there was little commercial fishing. The Gulf of Carpentaria Prawn Survey was its real commencement and the East Coast Prawn Fishery was in its early, small boat stage. Few trawlers exceeded 45ft. in length and most used a single net rig.

Why, during my twelve and a quarter years in charge of Fisheries, was I unable to recruit adequate research and technical staff, and lose my Fisheries Inspectors, when in the years after my demotion there was a rapid increase in Fisheries staff, and a huge increase in the status of Fisheries from a mere Branch to full departmental status as the Department of Primary Industries and Fisheries?

Steven Wardill, State Political Editor, wrote in "The Courier Mail" on 17th July 2010:

> "The Budget Estimates hearings are in dire need of reform. While there are fewer stunts now than in the past, the format still inhibits scrutiny.

> Ministers have to be asked all the questions, government committee chair-people protect them from the probing of the Opposition and strict time limits are set on each portfolio area.

> Some ministers even blatantly admit that their offices write the questions asked by Government MPs.

> It is a far cry from the system envisaged by the Goss government when it was introduced in 1994.

> The reforms needed are relatively minor but take a lot of political courage.

> Committees should not be dominated by the Government and should be chaired by Independent MPs, if possible.

> And senior public servants should be made to answer questions.

> It's done that way in Canberra.

> Why can't it happen in Queensland?"

CHAPTER 23

THE LONG ROAD TO JUSTICE

I suffered countless years of humiliation, criticism and embarrassment. I lost my promotional prospects, my career, and my professional reputation at a national and an international level. I was denied the opportunity to defend myself. Fisheries Minister, the Hon. Claude Wharton, confirmed to me that my efforts to develop Queensland Fisheries were blocked. He said that if I were to be re-appointed I would continue to be blocked.

In my view, the establishment of the Queensland Fisheries Service was used as a means to remove me and to enable the promotion of …(name supplied). It was not set up to manage Queensland Fisheries as I had intended. He was supported by his friends in the Queensland Public Service (club). I was in the way.

When I recommended the new Fisheries organisation, which became the Queensland Fisheries Service, I made my greatest blunder. I supplied the opportunity for new non-appealable posts to be created.

Taxpayers' money would have been more productive if spent on infrastructure, which is proving so costly now, rather than waging a personal vendetta against me for many years.

I lost a great deal of my superannuation entitlements. A circular was sent to the Department of Primary Industries head office notifying employees of the opportunity to buy extra units in order to increase their superannuation package. I was not located in the head office of DPI as I was in a separate building, where I was the only person affected by the circular. As I travelled in my job it was some considerable time before I saw the circular, by accident, and when I applied I was out of time, although when I was appointed in 1963 I made it very clear that I wanted the full number of superannuation units.

I approached the Superannuation Office who made representations to the Solicitor-General's Office on my behalf, but on a false premise by saying that I had tried to buy extra units from 1982, whereas I sought to buy extra units only after 1992, following the introduction of Freedom of Information.

Although I have resided at my current address since coming to Queensland in 1963, I very nearly missed out a second time when the Merry Widows' Scheme was announced. I happened to read about it in the press, but I was not contacted by the Government Superannuation Office.

It was reported in "The Courier-Mail" 6th December 2002:

Bureaucrats overpaid 4 million dollars

"Queensland public servants were overpaid more that 4 million dollars last financial year, an audit has revealed. Almost 2 million dollars worth of the money remains unaccounted for after being wrongly paid to bureaucrats in 30 departments'."

I was never invited to participate in any of the meetings of the Queensland Commercial Fishermen's Organisation, although I supported the fishermen in having it established, and it took me three attempts before the Government finally approved its establishment.

I had made several approaches before going to the United Kingdom on long service leave in 1976 to attend a conference on the processing of tropical fish – a field in which I am an expert – which I felt would be useful for Queensland. My fare had already been paid by me. After many requests I was never given permission to attend, nor was my written application officially acknowledged. All I was told was that my home telephone was not regarded as official any more.

A letter dated 3rd January 1965, was sent to me by the addressee signed … (Name supplied). It was stated in this letter, inter alia:

"At the time Harrison was out on the Swains with Tom Hiley, their wives and families, doing a very official Fisheries survey of the place. Wonder who paid for it? You may have had some mention of it up there; it was aboard one of the Roylen boats. I now find they never even got into the Swains; their guide apparently took them to the outskirts, took one horrified look at the channel country and the tide-rips, and that was that. I had wondered just who could have been competent to take the Ministerial party into that wasteland……………,someone has been tipping the papers "Strewth" off about the Ministers going out fishing in Departmental launches."

Who was white-anting my wife and family?

My wife and family have never been to the Swains Reef area. The truth of the matter is that Sir Thomas Hiley, Minister responsible for Fisheries, wished to inspect the coral reef fishery. Therefore, he chartered a Roylen cruiser, invited Dr. Geoff Kesteven, Chief of the CSIRO Fisheries Division, and me to join him in a tour of inspection of the Swains Reefs area. Commercial fishing in this area had been pioneered by Snowy Maltman, who owned and operated a vessel called the "Reef Queen". He fished often in the rip country on the outside of the Swains Reef area. Sir Thomas Hiley arranged for Snowy Maltman to accompany the party as a pilot. The two vacant cabins on the vessel were occupied by Alan Sewell, Under-Treasurer, and Sir Thomas Hiley's son.

Dr. Kesteven and I recorded the catches from each area, including the rip country.

Waste, duplication, overlapping, Empire-building, toadyism/ cronyism, professional jealousy and excessive lurks and perks should be eliminated from our system of Government. The creation of new jobs for those who fail, or to push somebody sideways, or to corner them, should be removed.

I am at a loss to understand why, generally speaking, in our system of Democracy, it is the victims who are punished and lose everything, whilst the perpetrators are promoted.

I believe my unique story, captured in this book, needed to be recorded.

The important series of events, which occurred during this time, commenced with the retirement of Sir Thomas Hiley, Premier Sir Francis (Frank) Nicklin and the premature death of his successor Premier Jack Pizzey. During their reign the Government and the Public Service served Queensland well.

I served under Premier Johannes Bjelke-Petersen from 1968.

It was recorded in "The Courier-Mail" 22nd October 1970, inter alia that:

"… the Premier's (Mr. Joh Bjelke-Petersen) opponents planned to install the Lands Minister, Mr. Sullivan, as Deputy Leader.

Last night Liberal and Country Party members were convinced that there must be another challenge because such a large section of the Parliamentary Party was openly committed against the Premier.

Mr. Bjelke-Petersen is understood to have sought an open vote on a show of hands.

Mr. Ahern, Landsborough, called for a secret ballot and Premier Bjelke-Petersen finally agreed. The vote, including some proxies from absent members, resulted in 11 all. Premier Bjelke-Petersen then produced two proxies he had been holding to produce the result 13-11, including his own vote.

Some disappointed Country Party members claimed that one of the Proxies held by the Premier was from a member who had reversed his decision by telegram only yesterday morning".

"The Courier-Mail" of 24th October 1970, indicated that two proxies were from Mr. Hewitt (Mackenzie) signed by a female, and from Mr. Hungerford (Balonne) proxy on a proxy.

As already mentioned, I never had the opportunity to speak to Premier Joh Bjelke-Petersen about Fisheries. When Fisheries problems arose in the early days, Premier Nicklin, Minister Hiley and Premier Pizzey each called me in for advice. During the reign of Premier Bjelke-Petersen I was an "Outsider" and many of my plans were blocked by bureaucratic delays. It took me a long time to find the source of my problems and to discover that I had no power to deal with them. I was in Queensland for about five years before I realised there was a "Public Service Club" which, based on my experience, looked after its members.

'Honest Cop' Ray Whitrod tried to stamp out corruption with his steadfast efforts, but he lost the battle after seven years.

The Fitzgerald Enquiry lasted for two years and sought to restore democracy to the Queensland political scene. Many reforms and new legislation were introduced. The Hon. Mike Ahern was a distinguished Premier and he was able to start Queensland on its return to democracy, in spite of the baggage he inherited.

Premier Wayne Goss was recognised as a reformer, particularly electoral honesty and accountability. He had his critics in the manner in which he handled the Koala Road, and in scrapping the Wolfdene Dam.

During the reign of Premier Joh Bjelke-Petersen, the Public Service was rapidly politicised. The Police Force was transformed. The process of creating and appointing quangos and other unelected authorities waxed rampant, in order to provide the means of hiding political ineptitude and corruption.

Sure, the cranes worked hard, but at what cost?

My story shows how these malpractices can develop for personal reasons, or through old-fashioned cronyism, and cost the community dearly. I could see what was happening at the time, and could do nothing to help.

I have sought redress through every possible avenue available to me in the search for justice for the taxpayer and for me, not only through the media and the legal fraternity, but to no avail.

Democratic Government exists **for the public**, not for some senior bureaucrats, unelected and unaccountable –

Government Of The People
Government By The People
Government For The People.

"The Courier-Mail" reported on Monday, 15th February 2010, inter alia:

"In the pre-Fitzgerald 1980s, the focus was on Fortitude Valley. Now "sin city" has shifted to the Gold Coast. When combined with revelations from the Crime and Misconduct Commission's Dangerous Liaison's report from last year, Queenslanders could be forgiven for thinking that the State has indeed gone back to the bad old days, as some commentators suggest.

But, as anti-corruption Commissioner Tony Fitzgerald noted last year, vigilance is needed to maintain the reform agenda in the face of complacency and self-interest.

It is easy to forget the scale and reach of the corruption that Fitzgerald uncovered.

The biggest disappointment has been the continued failure to achieve real reform of Parliament. The goal was an active and informed check on executive power but the reality has been political posturing and often inane debate.

Improving integrity among ministers and senior public officers has also been a difficult target."

It was reported in "The Courier-Mail" on 3rd March 2010, inter alia, as follows:

"The man who blew the lid off Queensland's political corruption in the 1980s says the State's Labor Government has been descending into cronyism and bad practice.

After an "auspicious" start with a reform agenda, Labor is now taking the opportunity to give its supporters their turn at the trough, retired Judge, Tony Fitzgerald, said at the launch of a biography on former Liberal leader Terry White yesterday.

Queensland is no longer the isolated deep north, but is now in the mainstream of political malpractice.

Between 1987 and 1989 Mr. Fitzgerald conducted an inquiry that revealed the extent of political and police corruption in Queensland under the government of Sir Joh Bjelke-Petersen..........".

It was reported in "The Courier-Mail" on the 12th March 2010 inter alia:

"Anti-corruption crusader Tony Fitzgerald has used his "last public statement" to slam Australia's political culture as one controlled by money, lacking in ethics and riddled with secrecy and misinformation.

The former royal commissioner who lifted the lid on political and police corruption in Queensland in the 1980s made the scathing remarks at the launch of a new award for parliamentary integrity in Melbourne yesterday.

Mr. Fitzgerald said the concept of ministerial responsibility was now obsolescent.

"The prevailing political culture is increasingly amoral with each party lowering its standards, exploiting gaps in the law and disregarding ethical standards in order to compete," Mr. Fitzgerald said.

"Whatever it takes. Winner takes all."

Mr. Fitzgerald said the halls of power were dominated by careerists with little or no experience outside politics and those who "learn their craft in party administration, politician's offices and supporter's organisations."

When asked if he thought whether Australia was broken, he said: "No, it's bent."

CHAPTER 24

'IT'S OUR SYSTEM THAT IS STUFFED'

"The Courier-Mail", 6th August 2010

"The way Queensland is governed and managed – its governance and infrastructure – is in urgent need of a major overhaul writes Scott Prasser. Professor Scott Prassar is executive director of the Public Policy Institute of the Australian Catholic Institute.

Most think about Queensland's infrastructure crisis only in terms of inadequate roads, dams, schools, power stations, public transport and traffic congestion. Poor planning, lack of funding and delayed decision-making, are usually blamed for this mess. That's only half-right. The real culprit is Queensland's other infrastructure crisis, our governance infrastructure: our parliamentary institutions, election processes, the public service, the judiciary system, government business enterprises, our political parties and the way we develop and deliver policy.

They do not work any more. They are out of date, ossified and manipulated by whoever is in power to maintain office rather than to reflect democratic will or to be accountable to the electorate.

The electorate may vote every three years but between elections voters have few mechanisms to hold government to account or to force it out of office for its ineptitude.

Look at how the current Government failed to inform the electorate in the 2009 election about privatisation. The lack of consultation is as bad as the Beattie government's enforced local government amalgamation.

Look at the overseas doctors' scandal. People die in Queensland's public hospitals, but not one minister has been sacked; a man dies in a police lock-up on Palm Island and not one minister has taken responsibility and resigned.
We cannot even pay staff in public hospitals, but no minister has been dismissed.

Millions of taxpayers' dollars have been squandered on "white-elephant" projects that were never properly costed, and failed to deliver – a magnesium project that lost millions, the proposed Traveston Dam, the Gold Coast's desalination plant, the Indy car debacle and tunnels with few cars.

And yet we have no parliamentary committee or independent inquiries into any of these debacles. Just a few post-event reports by the Auditor-General, who tells us the obvious – processes and planning were poor or virtually non-existent.

Our present system of governance has broken down. Our parliamentary system is Westminster gone troppo.

Parliament only sits 50 days a year. The governing party controls all its procedures. Question time is a farce, legislation is rushed and the Opposition, inept as it is, neutered.

Queensland's single house parliamentary system makes it worse. An upper house, if properly constructed, might exert restraint on the present excesses of executive government, ensure more consultation and provide better representation for regions or other groups. But it has been ruled out by the current Government in its response to the Integrity and Accountability discussion paper last year.

Another problem is the crisis in the level of talent among our elected officials. Political parties are suffering from declining memberships and their own gene pool is contracting. Fewer of our elected officials are from the broader community.

More of them have had only limited careers or work experience outside their own parties, which, in turn, have ceased to be representative of the electorate. So let's consider other methods of recruiting into the ministry the best and brightest that our society has rather than just relying on those of one political allegiance.

This means a fundamental change to Westminster government, but Westminster is not working in Queensland, so let's do it.

Then there is our public service. It has grown too much and has become increasingly politicised during the past two decades. It has lost any semblance of independence and the quality of its advice has declined. It has become too responsive to the whims of elected officials.

Even Queensland Treasury is a pushover these days as Queensland's growing herd of white-elephant projects, deficit fiscal situation and declining credit rating testify.

Unlike Canberra we do not have the independent advisory bodies that provide the analysis that we all can see. We need a

State Priorities Commission to identify key infrastructure needs based on publicly released cost-benefit studies and with open consultation.

Where is Queensland's intergenerational report on our ageing population and its policy impact for the future? Do we have to wait for another crisis? The present Planning Information and Forecasting Unit has done great work on population issues but is now buried in State Treasury. It should be an external independent body so we can see all the evidence and hear its unfiltered views on population trends.

Voters also want more direct means to input into decision-making, not sham consultations about decisions already made. Community cabinets had some impact, but more substantial changes are required. That means opening up the decision-making processes and devolving responsibility to local communities.

We could start with a parliamentary committee on education to consider community input on our school curriculums.

We could have more community ownership of public schools.

We could promote more open and competitive arrangements in the delivery of a whole range of public policies, from education to infrastructure.

Queensland needs a new public service that is re-professionalised (not re-structured) and insulated from political interference but accountable through annual reporting to independent boards of management about specified performance targets.

This means a revitalised and independent Public Service Commission to manage the integrity of the system and public and bipartisan scrutiny of senior appointments to the bureaucracy, government boards and the judiciary.

Queensland will soon have lots of shiny new infrastructure. But to get the most out of it we need a new governance infrastructure based on the solid foundations of democratic practice, transparency and maximum citizen involvement.

With fewer constitutional limitations than at the federal level, there is no reason why Queensland cannot lead in this process of government renewal. We need to start now. It needs to happen at a state level."

I recall a conversation I had with Mr. Jim Houghton MP, in 1970, at the opening of the Deception Bay Laboratory, wherein he said that the Queensland Government system was not working satisfactorily, and needed to be changed.

It's time.

DEMonOCRACY?

Under the United Nations Charter I was entitled to just and favourable conditions of work, but this did not apply to me in Queensland.

The following is an extract in part of an article that appeared in "The Courier-Mail" on 27th September 2010 by Stefanie Balogh, National Political Correspondent:

> "Catholic Health Australia chief executive Martin Laverty said international evidence says 'your education or job is more important to your health than cholesterol, blood pressure and smoking combined'."

My two former assistants, Ernest Morgan Grant and Noel Melville Haysom, retired senior to me, although one was holding an unclassified position and the other was only on a temporary appointment when I took charge of Fisheries – I took action to have them appointed to a scientific grade in the Public Service in which they would have promotion prospects.

I am a practising Catholic, and I have never been a member of any Political Party. I did my duty with a real desire to serve Queensland.

The Harrison Family at Manly in 2017.

ABOUT THE AUTHOR

Geoff Harrison was born in 1922 and raised in York, England. During World War II, he served for five years in the Royal Air Force and the Homeguard, prior to joining the Colonial Service in West Africa. As a Radar Instructor-Mechanic, his RAF service was classified 'top secret'.

Following his war service, Geoff attended the University of Leeds and graduated with a Bachelor of Science (Chemistry). He completed training courses in Fisheries Management in Denmark conducted by the Food and Agriculture Organisation of the United Nations as well as courses in food canning, echo sounders and marine engines in the United Kingdom.

Joining the Colonial Service in 1949, Geoff served in the Department of Fisheries in Ghana for thirteen years, the last three years as Chief Fisheries Officer. During this time, he became the pioneer of what was to become the world's biggest tuna fishery. With the help of the American company StarKist Seafoods, Geoff was able to grow the fishery in Ghana which then spread through the Gulf of Guinea.

It was in Ghana that Geoff met Eunice Enright. Eunice was from Queensland and at that time was working for the Australian High Commission. They married in England in 1961 but chose to make Queensland home. They started married life in Manly overlooking Moreton Bay, raised four children and continue to live in the same family home 56 years later.

The decision to make Queensland home coincided with Geoff's acceptance to take on the job of Chief Inspector of Fisheries and Senior Biologist (Queensland), the most senior Fisheries Officer in Queensland. His task was to put all Fisheries matters, except the Fish Board, under the one umbrella, for the first time.

Printed in Great Britain
by Amazon

44785723R00102